P9-ELP-763

ANDREW JOHNSON

REBUILDING THE UNION

THE HISTORY OF THE CIVIL WAR

THE HISTORY OF THE CIVIL WAR

ANDREW JOHNSON

REBUILDING THE UNION

by CATHY EAST DUBOWSKI

INTRODUCTORY ESSAY BY
HENRY STEELE COMMAGER

SILVER BURDETT PRESS

Series Editorial Supervisor: Richard G. Gallin
Series Editing: Agincourt Press
Series Consultant: Leah Fortson
Cover and Text Design: Circa 86, Inc.
Series Supervision of Art and Design: Leslie Bauman
Maps: Susan Johnston Carlson

Consultants: Richard M. Haynes, Assistant Professor, Division of
Administration, Curriculum, and Instruction, Western Carolina
University; Karen E. Markoe, Professor of History, Maritime
College of the State University of New York.

Library of Congress Cataloging-in-Publication Data

Dubowski, Cathy East.
    Andrew Johnson : rebuilding the union / by Cathy East Dubowski;
    introduction by Henry Steele Commager
        p.   cm. — (The History of the Civil War)
    Includes bibliographical references and index.
    Summary: Surveys the political career and private life of the only
president ever to be impeached.
    1. Johnson, Andrew, 1809–1875—Juvenile literature.
    2. Presidents—United States—Biography—Juvenile literature.
    3. Reconstruction—Juvenile literature.   4. United States—Politics
and government—1865–1869—Juvenile literature. [1.Johnson,
Andrew, 1809–1875. 2. Presidents.] I. Title. II. Series.
    E667.D88   1991
    973.5′6′092—dc20
    [B]
    [92]   90-25650
    ISBN 0-382-09945-1 (LSB) : ISBN 0-382-24054-5 (pbk.)   CIP
                                                               AC

TABLE OF CONTENTS

HENRY STEELE COMMAGER

Andrew Johnson's life is an example of the classic "rags to riches story" so popular in American politics. The irony is that though he did rise from obscurity, he is one of the least well known of our nation's presidents.

He was born in North Carolina—into a society that kept slaves—but did not himself own slaves or approve of slavery. Early on he moved to Tennessee, where he made a difficult living as apprentice to a tailor. While listening to books being read aloud to amuse the workers, he became fascinated by politics. He taught himself to read, and took an active part in local politics. In time, he raised a family of five, and proved to be a powerful speaker.

Eventually Johnson ran for statewide office—always championing the interests of the small farmer and working man. Soon he was mayor of his town of Greeneville. His ambitions grew with success: he was elected to the state legislature, then to the U.S. Congress. In time, Johnson became a national figure.

After losing his seat in the Senate, Johnson became governor of Tennessee. In this office Johnson concentrated on state aid to education and to workers and farmers. This progressive legislation brought him national attention.

Then came the Civil War. The war was preceded by a great crisis over the question of whether states could break away from the Union. Johnson stood openly by the Union—a decision that commended him to the new Republican party. In contrast with many other Southern politicians, Johnson believed the Union should be indivisible, that it was not possible for states to secede.

It was Johnson's defense of the Union that persuaded the Republican party, in 1864, to nominate him as Abraham Lincoln's running mate in the presidential election.

Johnson was largely responsible for keeping Tennessee in the Union (though part of it did go with the Confederacy). As vice-president, Johnson contributed little to running the war, but after the assassination of Lincoln, the fact that there was a southerner in the White House made an important difference.

Johnson did carry on much of Lincoln's policy of reconciliation with the South. It is worth remembering that no other civil war was ever concluded with so little punishment or so much generosity as that between the Union and the Confederacy.

President Johnson may not be well remembered, but his position in history was certainly remarkable. Without his loyalty, the Union might not have held, and certainly without his work it might never have gotten back together.

CIVIL WAR TIME LINE

May 22
Kansas-Nebraska Act states that in new territories the question of slavery will be decided by the citizens. Many Northerners are outraged because this act could lead to the extension of slavery.

| 1854 | 1855 | 1856 | 1857 |

May 21
Lawrence, Kansas is sacked by proslavery Missourians.
May 22
Senator Charles Sumner is caned by Preston Brooks for delivering a speech against slavery.
May 24 – 25
Pottawatomie Creek massacre committed by John Brown and four of his sons.

March 6
The Supreme Court, in the *Dred Scott* ruling, declares that blacks are not U. S. citizens, and therefore cannot bring lawsuits. The ruling divides the country on the question of the legal status of blacks.

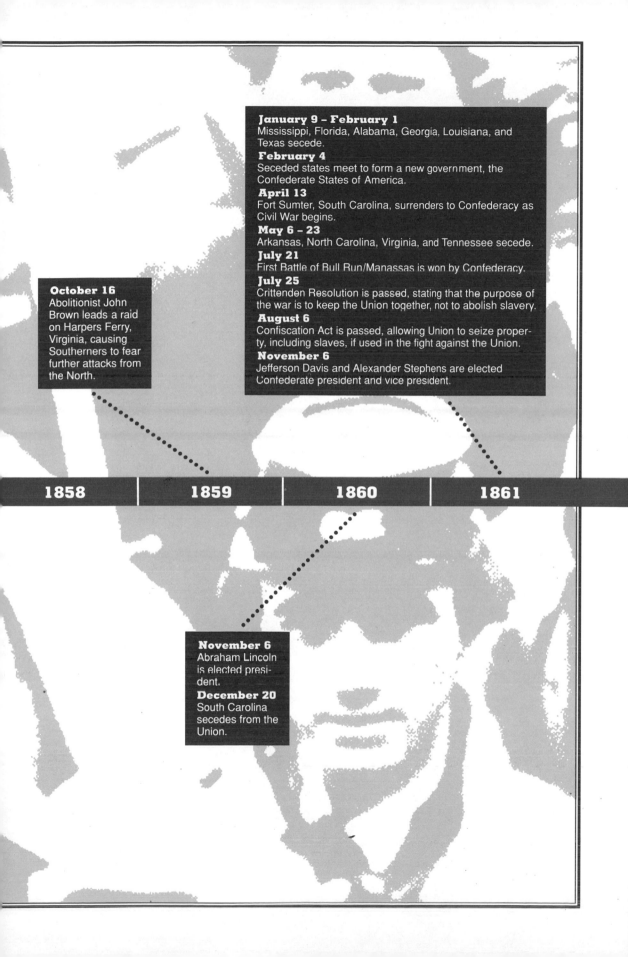

January 9 – February 1
Mississippi, Florida, Alabama, Georgia, Louisiana, and Texas secede.

February 4
Seceded states meet to form a new government, the Confederate States of America.

April 13
Fort Sumter, South Carolina, surrenders to Confederacy as Civil War begins.

May 6 – 23
Arkansas, North Carolina, Virginia, and Tennessee secede.

July 21
First Battle of Bull Run/Manassas is won by Confederacy.

July 25
Crittenden Resolution is passed, stating that the purpose of the war is to keep the Union together, not to abolish slavery.

August 6
Confiscation Act is passed, allowing Union to seize property, including slaves, if used in the fight against the Union.

November 6
Jefferson Davis and Alexander Stephens are elected Confederate president and vice president.

October 16
Abolitionist John Brown leads a raid on Harpers Ferry, Virginia, causing Southerners to fear further attacks from the North.

1858   **1859**   **1860**   **1861**

November 6
Abraham Lincoln is elected president.

December 20
South Carolina secedes from the Union.

February 6
Fort Henry, Tennessee, is captured.

February 16
Fort Donelson, Tennessee, is captured by Union.

March 9
Monitor and *Merrimack* battle near Hampton Roads, Virginia.

March 23
Shenandoah Valley Campaign opens with Union victory over Maj. Gen. Thomas J. "Stonewall" Jackson.

April 7
Gen. Ulysses S. Grant wins Battle of Shiloh, Tennessee, splitting rebel forces on the Mississippi River.

April 25
New Orleans is captured by Union naval forces led by flag officer David Farragut.

June 19
Slavery is abolished in U. S. territories.

June 25
Gen. Robert E. Lee leads rout of Gen. George McClellan's army in the Seven Days Battles.

July 17
The United States Congress authorizes formation of the first black regiments.

August 29 – 30
Second Battle of Bull Run/Manassas is won by Confederacy.

September 5
Lee leads first Confederate invasion of the North into Maryland.

September 17
Battle of Antietam/Sharpsburg, bloodiest of the war, ends in a stalemate between Lee and McClellan.

1862 **1863** **1864** **1865**

January 1
Lincoln issues Emancipation Proclamation, freeing slaves in Confederate states.

March 3
U.S. Congress passes its first military draft.

April 2
Bread riots occur in Richmond, Virginia.

May 1 – 4
Battle of Chancellorsville is won by Confederacy; Stonewall Jackson is accidentally shot by his own troops.

May 22 – July 4
Union wins siege of Vicksburg in Mississippi.

June 3
Lee invades the North from Fredericksburg, Virginia.

July 3
Battle of Gettysburg is won in Pennsylvania by Union.

July 13 – 17
Riots occur in New York City over the draft.

November 19
Lincoln delivers the Gettysburg Address.

March 12
Grant becomes general-in-chief of Union army.

May 5 – 6
Lee and Lt. Gen. James Longstreet defeat Grant at the Wilderness Battle in Virginia.

May 6 – September 2
Atlanta Campaign ends in Union general William Tecumseh Sherman's occupation of Atlanta.

May 8 – 19
Lee and Grant maneuver for position in the Spotsylvania Campaign.

June 3
Grant is repelled at Cold Harbor, Virginia.

June 18, 1864 – April 2, 1865
Grant conducts the Siege of Petersburg, in Virginia, ending with evacuation of the city and Confederate withdrawal from Richmond.

August 5
Admiral Farragut wins Battle of Mobile Bay for Union.

October 6
Union general Philip Sheridan lays waste to Shenandoah Valley, Virginia, cutting off Confederacy's food supplies.

November 8
Lincoln is reelected president.

November 15 – December 13
Sherman's March to the Sea ends with Union occupation of Savannah, Georgia

March 2
First Reconstruction Act is passed, reorganizing governments of Southern states.

1866   **1867**   **1868**   **1869**

April 9
Civil Rights Act of 1866 is passed. Among other things, it removes states' power to keep former slaves from testifying in court or owning property.

November 3
Ulysses S. Grant is elected president.

January 31
Thirteenth Amendment, freeing slaves, is passed by Congress and sent to states for ratification.

February 1 – April 26
Sherman invades the Carolinas.

February 6
Lee is appointed general-in-chief of Confederate armies.

March 3
Freedman's Bureau is established to assist former slaves.

April 9
Lee surrenders to Grant at Appomattox Courthouse, Virginia.

April 15
Lincoln dies from assassin's bullet; Andrew Johnson becomes president.

May 26
Remaining Confederate troops surrender.

A Poor Apprentice

"If being poor was a crime...I should have to plead that I was guilty: and that I had lived a criminal a large portion of my life."

ANDREW JOHNSON, SPEAKING TO HIS FELLOW CONGRESSMEN ABOUT HIS YOUTH

Decembcr 29, 1808, was a dark, cold night in Raleigh, the capital of North Carolina. But just across from the State House, in Casso's Inn, the windows were ablaze with candlelight. A joyful Christmas-week ball filled the night with light and laughter, fiddling and singing.

Owner Peter Casso was a former Revolutionary soldier. His inn was the finest in thc rcgion and boasted some 25 beds, 4 huge fireplaces, and a well-stocked bar. The inn was often filled with legislators and lawyers, aristocrats and well-dressed travelers. It was a crossroads in a young town in a new nation.

Some say it was a memorable night because it was the wedding ball of Peter Casso's daughter, "Pretty Peggy." But something even more memorable had happened in a tiny two-story wooden house that sat in the inn's backyard.

A poor uneducated woman was in the small upstairs bedroom that made up the entire upper floor of the house. She must have heard the laughter and music through the single dormer window as she labored to give birth. At last, late in the dark night, her child was born—a son.

Some say that Casso's daughter hurried across the cold dark yard and into the little cabin to see the new baby. Some even say that the well-dressed, aristocratic young lady suggested the name Andrew.

Who among them could have guessed the squalling baby's future? Who among the merrymakers, the servants, or the child's own family could have guessed that the woman held in her arms the 17th president of the United States?

Andrew Johnson's parents were poor, uneducated working folks. Neither could read or write. Andy's father, Jacob Johnson, was born in England and came to America in 1795. His wanderings brought him to Raleigh, where he met and married Mary McDonough "Polly" Johnson. Polly Johnson worked washing and mending legislators' clothes. Jacob worked at odd jobs. He sometimes worked as a porter at Casso's Inn. Sometimes he filled in as sexton at the Presbyterian church and rang the town's only bell, which stood in Casso's courtyard, for weddings, funerals, and

Highlights in the Life of Andrew Johnson

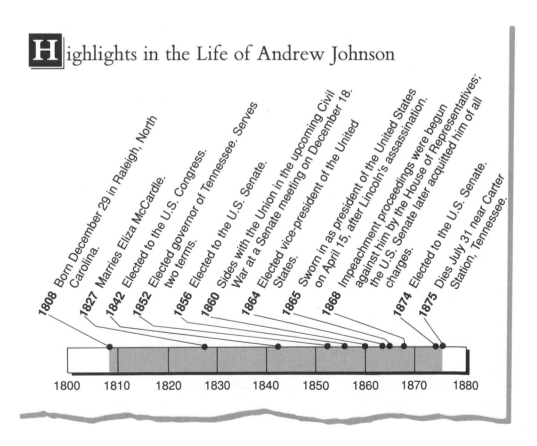

1808 Born December 29 in Raleigh, North Carolina.

1827 Marries Eliza McCardle.

1842 Elected to the U.S. Congress.

1852 Elected governor of Tennessee. Serves two terms.

1856 Elected to the U.S. Senate.

1860 Sides with the Union in the upcoming Civil War at a Senate meeting on December 18.

1864 Elected vice-president of the United States.

1865 Sworn in as president of the United States on April 15, after Lincoln's assassination.

1868 Impeachment proceedings were begun against him by the House of Representatives; the U.S. Senate later acquitted him of all charges.

1874 Elected to the U.S. Senate.

1875 Dies July 31 near Carter Station, Tennessee.

1800   1810   1820   1830   1840   1850   1860   1870   1880

fires. In 1811, he was hired as porter at the state bank of North Carolina. Together, Jacob and Polly Johnson just managed to put food on their family's table.

In December 1811, right before Andy's third birthday, tragedy struck. Jacob went along with "a merry party" to Hunter's Mill Pond—perhaps he had been hired to handle the food and clean the fish. At one point, three men—including Colonel Thomas Henderson, editor and publisher of the *Raleigh Star*—pushed off in a canoe onto Walnut Creek. The men were having a grand time, horsing around—until one of them tipped the boat. All three men plunged into the 10-foot deep waters. One made it to shore. Another man, who could not swim, grabbed onto Henderson. Both were in danger of drowning.

On shore, Jacob Johnson heard their cries for help. Without a thought, Johnson dived into the icy river. Soon he had managed to drag the men safely to shore.

Jacob Johnson had saved their lives. But he himself suffered from exhaustion and exposure. His health was ruined. Less than a month later, while ringing the town bell for a funeral, he collapsed. Soon after, he died.

On January 12, 1812, Henderson wrote in the *Star*:

> Died, in this city on Saturday last, Jacob Johnson, who for many years occupied a humble but useful station.... In his last illness he was visited by the principal inhabitants of the city, by all of whom he was esteemed for his honesty, sobriety, industry, and his humane, friendly disposition. Among all among whom he was known and esteemed, none lament him, except perhaps his own relatives, more than the publisher of this newspaper, for he owes his life on a particular occasion to the boldness and humanity of Johnson.

Jacob Johnson was buried in the "citizens' cemetery"—where they buried people who were so poor they could not pay for a burial spot. Polly could not even afford a simple stone. But 50 years later, a monument was erected that read: "In memory of Jacob Johnson. An honest man, loved and respected by all who knew him."

Polly Johnson was left with no husband, no money, and two small boys, William, eight, and Andy, just barely three. There was no life insurance money, and there were no government agencies to help the poor. Polly took up spinning and weaving and soon became known as "Polly the Weaver." She worked hard and long, but still could just barely feed her family. Years later, Andrew Johnson would remember, "Yes, I have wrestled with poverty, that gaunt and haggard monster. I have met it in the day and night. I have felt his withering approach and his blighting influence."

Raleigh was a town of barely a thousand people. Some 700 were white, 300 were black—270 of them slaves. Growing up, young Andy must have quickly grasped the stark class divisions that separated the town. Grand homes surrounded by lush gardens lined many of the well-planned streets. Well-dressed ladies and gentlemen dashed around town in expensive carriages drawn by the finest horses. Andy grew up resenting the rich for their unearned luxury and the blacks for the competition they offered the working man.

When Andy was a boy, there was virtually no middle class. Most people in Raleigh fell into one of three classes: wealthy aristocracy, poor whites—or black slaves. Less than 30 percent of Americans fell into the first, wealthy class. As for the second class, known as "poor whites," "mudsills," or plebeians, they were the laborers, or "have-nots." They worked for those who had, as farm workers, blacksmiths, cooks, or tailors. The slaves, the third class, had nothing. It was this difference—between very little and nothing—that distinguished the slaves from the poor whites.

At last, in 1814, Polly married a man named Turner Dougherty. But if she had hoped to improve her lot, she was certainly disappointed. Her new husband had trouble finding work—and trouble keeping a job. So the family was no better off than before.

Free public education was still a new idea, and Raleigh did not have a free school. Schools were by "subscription"—parents had to pay tuition to the teachers. So Andy and his brother Bill could not even go to school. In fact, Andy would never go to school a day in his life.

Few opportunities were available for people like the Johnsons. With no land, no money, and no education, there was little hope for Bill and Andy. Polly, however, was determined to do the best she could for her children. So when Bill turned 14, Polly arranged for him to become apprenticed to Colonel Henderson, the newspaperman whom Jacob Johnson had saved from drowning.

In the early 1800s, becoming an apprentice was one way for a poor boy to learn a trade. His master would give him food, clothes, and a place to sleep. In exchange, the boy agreed to work long hours for his master—and expect not one penny in wages—until he "came of age" at 21. Then the young man was free to earn a living at his new trade.

A good apprenticeship could be a fine start in life for a boy who had nothing. But is was not a casual arrangement. If a boy discovered he did not like the work, neither he nor his family could change their minds. The agreement between master and apprentice was a binding, legal contract. The boy had no freedom, and he must obey his master completely. If he had a good master, he was lucky and he learned a good trade. If he had a bad master, he had to learn to make the best of it. For being an apprentice was like being the master's property. It was almost like being a slave, although an apprentice could at least look forward to the day he earned his freedom.

Bill Johnson might have done well as a printer's apprentice. A year later, however, Colonel Henderson died and the contract ended. The town tailor, James Selby, agreed to take Bill into his busy shop.

J. Selby's was a large, busy workshop a block from the State Capitol building. Aristocrats and state officials waited in fine leather chairs or posed before a tall three-way mirror to inspect the fit of their fashionable new clothes.

Rolls and rolls of the finest tweeds and silks filled the shelves that lined the shop's large workroom. At the front table, a cloth cutter sat and chalked out the patterns of garments on the fabric. Then he passed the rough-cut cloth to the journeyman and the young apprentice tailors who sat on workbenches behind him. They in turn stitched the pieces into garments.

Master Selby sat a cluttered rolltop desk in the corner, barking out orders to sweep the floor or fetch more wood for the two small stoves. Often a person was hired to read to the workers from newspapers and books to help them pass the long hours.

When Andy heard about this from his older brother, he began to hang about the shop to hear the stories. A journeyman named Tom Lumsden said that Andy "was always pestering me out of work hours to read to him. He was a pert sort of boy, and one fall business was brisk, and the boss wanted a 'prentice. He took in Andy, and the boy was right glad to get something to do to help his old mother."

So 13-year-old Andy Johnson sat with the other apprentices for hours at a time and learned the tailor's trade. The hours were long, and the work was sometimes tedious. Bill was not very happy sitting hunched over a needle and thread while the sounds of other children playing drifted through the cracks in the windows.

Andy, however, seemed to take to it much better. Though he was a lively young boy, he had a steadfastness that saw him through the longest days. The shop's foreman, James Litchford, took quite a liking to the boy. He described Andy as "a wild, harum-scarum boy with no unhonorable traits, however." He learned to make straight, sure stitches. He learned how to set a coat sleeve, iron a seam, and turn odd shapes of cloth into a garment a gentleman was proud to wear on the finest occasion.

But more than anything, it was the reading that held Andy Johnson fast to his seat.

Dr. William G. Hill—otherwise known as Bill Hill—was coming to the shop now to read. An intellectual with a fine voice, he often read from *The American Speaker*, a collection of great speeches by American and British statesmen. Often the shop was

William Pitt, Earl of Chatham, whose speech on liberty inspired young Andrew Johnson.

filled with clients and passersby caught up in a lively discussion of ideas. The complex intellectual ideas must have been difficult for a young boy like Andy to understand at times. But for a boy who had been locked out of school because the price was too high, these stirring words were precious indeed. The book also included essays on how to be a good speaker. "Aim at nothing higher," it said, "till you can read distinctly and deliberately." Most important, it suggested:

Learn to speak slow, all other graces
Will follow in the proper places.

Andy was so taken with the book, in fact, that he begged to borrow it. Instead, Bill Hill gave him a copy of his very own.

The weeks and months passed. By day, Andy sat cross-legged in Selby's tailor shop for 12 hours a day. His fingers grew fast and sure with a needle and thread, and his mind grew sharp and quick and full of exciting ideas. He practiced speaking slowly and clearly. Sometimes Hill and Litchford helped him with his ABCs. By night, Andy struggled over the type in *The American Speaker*, puzzling out the words of some of the world's greatest thinkers. He was particularly impressed by speeches on liberty by England's William Pitt. Slowly, he taught himself to read. Suddenly a whole new world of ideas was open to this poor tailor's apprentice. A yearning for something beyond his own small world burned in his heart like wildfire.

The years of his apprenticeship stretched before him. It seemed like forever.

But it would not be.

RUNAWAY!

"TEN DOLLARS REWARD. Ran away from
the Subscriber, on the night of the 15th instant,
two apprentice boys, legally bound, named
WILLIAM AND ANDREW JOHNSON."
NOTICE IN THE RALEIGH *Gazette, June 24, 1824*

Unlike most of Selby's "bound boys," Andy did not live at
the shop. He was allowed to live at home, perhaps so he
could help his mother. So sometimes Andy found time to
stretch his legs in wild, free play with other town boys. And often
he led the crowd, whether it was roaming the forests, swimming in
the rivers, or climbing trees. He showed up at the tailor shop in
torn clothes so often that Mrs. Selby wore herself out scolding him.
At last she made him a coarse, heavy one-piece undergarment and
made him wear that!

When Andy was 15, he and some other "bound boys" got into
real trouble—when they got on the wrong side of a widow named
Mrs. Wells. The stories vary on exactly what happened. Some
biographers say that Mrs. Wells had insulted the boys and called
them "white trash." To pay her back, the boys rocked her house
back and forth on its foundation. Others say Andy and his friends
threw pieces of wood at her house. Still others say it was rocks they
threw—to attract the attention of Mrs. Well's pretty daughters. The
stories may differ—but Mrs. Well's angry reaction was clear. She
threatened to "persecute" the boys and have them thrown in jail.

It was not an empty threat from a cranky old lady. The law dealt harshly with apprentices who got into trouble. They could easily be thrown in jail. In the middle of the night, Andy, his brother Bill, and two other "bound boys" threw their few belongings in a cloth sack. Then they ran away.

James Selby was furious. He ran a notice in the Raleigh *Gazette*:

TEN DOLLARS REWARD.

Ran away from the Subscriber, on the night of the 15th instant, two apprentice boys, legally bound, named WILLIAM AND ANDREW JOHNSON. The former is of a dark complexion, black hair, eyes, and habits. They are much of a height, about 5 feet 4 or 5 inches. The latter is very fleshy, freckled face, light hair, and fair complexion. They went off with two other apprentices, advertised by Messrs. Wm. & Chas. Fowler. When they went away, they were well clad—blue cloth coats, light colored homespun coats, and new hats, the maker's name in the crown of the hats is, Theodore Clark. I will pay the above Reward to any person who will deliver said apprentices to me in Raleigh, or I will give the above Reward for Andrew Johnson alone.

　　All persons are cautioned against harboring or employing said apprentices, on pain of being prosecuted.

　　　　　　　　　　　　　　　　　　　—JAMES J. SELBY, Tailor

Raleigh, N.C., June 24, 1824

Clearly Selby thought the ungrateful boys had done him wrong. He must have been beside himself with anger—because he got the boys' descriptions backwards. In fact, Bill was the fair, freckle-faced boy. Andy had a dark complexion, striking black eyes, and dark black hair. And though Selby said the boy had "black habits," too, the tailor obviously placed a high value on his high-spirited apprentice—since he offered to pay the entire $10 dollar reward for Andy alone.

　　But the boys got away.

　　They did not stop running till they arrived tired and hungry in Carthage, North Carolina, some 75 miles away. Andy somehow rented a small shack and worked for the summer as a journeyman tailor. He was smart. He had learned his trade well. And he earned enough in this tiny village to get by. But as long as he was in North Carolina, he was still in danger of being caught and sent back to Selby—and certain punishment. Six months later, he fled across the state line to the town of Laurens, South Carolina.

　　Andy go a room at a hotel in Laurens and a job in a local tailor shop. The young tailor must have learned his trade well by now, for he was even chosen to sew the wedding coat of the town's schoolteacher. When he was not sewing, he had his nose in a book.

　　Andy was growing up. At 15 years old, he was on his own and earning his own way. Some time that winter, Andy fell in love.

　　Sarah Word was a shy, beautiful town girl about Andy's age. He helped her plan and make a quilt. He gave her his tailor's goose, a special iron with a long, curved goosenecked handle. Before the winter was over, he asked her parents for permission to marry her.

But Sarah's parents had higher hopes for their daughter. They did not want her to marry a wandering tailor with an uncertain future. Their answer was no.

Andy was broken-hearted. But he did not fight them on their decision. Soon he decided to leave Laurens. He and his brother decided to return to Raleigh and try to clear their names.

When they got to Raleigh, they found out that Selby had moved 20 miles out into the country. Selby's foreman, James Litchford, had opened his own tailor shop. Andy asked his old friend for a job. But Andy's apprenticeship with Selby still stood, and Litchford was afraid to hire a runaway. So Andy made up his mind. He walked the 20 miles to see Selby. He apologized and asked for his old job back. But Selby refused to have him without a large amount of money for security—in case he ran away again. Andy could not come up with that kind of money. The threat of jail still hung over his head.

Andy made up his mind. There was only one thing to do: He would have to leave North Carolina, his home.

One bright, moonlit night in August 1826, Andy Johnson threw a bundle of clothes over his shoulder. With one last, sad look around his hometown, he started walking west.

Andy's friend Tom Lumsden, a journeyman tailor, walked with him a mile or two out of town to see him off. "He was talking all the time about the great things he intended to do out West," Lumsden later remembered. "When he shook hands, and he bade me good-bye, the tears just rolled down his cheeks."

Lumsden tried to lighten the mood. "Cheer up, Andy," he told his friend. "Raleigh is no place for you." Then he added what many a young American boy was told in those days: "You'll succeed out there, and some day I hope to see you President, for you are bound to be a great man."

Lumsden had no way of knowing then just how true his words would one day turn out to be.

TENNESSEE TAILOR

"If you want a brand-new coat
   I'll tell you what to do:
   Go down to Andrew Johnson's shop
   And get a long tail blue."

CHILDREN'S SONG IN GREENEVILLE

Andrew Johnson—his pockets empty and his heart full of hope—headed out on foot for the Blue Ridge Mountains.

In the early years of the United States, the West was a symbol of opportunity. A chance for a young man with nothing to start from scratch—to make a life for himself with the hard work of his own two hands.

Andy hitched a ride whenever he could. He slept under the stars or asked folks along the way for a dry spot to lay his head for the night. Sometimes a kind individual would even send the skinny young boy off the next morning with a country breakfast under his belt.

One day Andy rested beside the road in his travel-dusted clothes, his small bundle of belongings at his feet. Along came a train of wagons carrying household goods and slaves. A rich Carolinian named Mr. Brown was moving to Tennessee.

Andy looked up shyly with his piercing black eyes. Climb aboard, Brown insisted. Soon Johnson was jostling along the rocky road in a covered wagon.

At last the wagon train reached Knoxville, Tennessee. Andy thanked Brown and then took a flatboat that was headed down the Tennessee and Little Tennessee rivers. When he reached Decatur, Alabama, he got out and looked for work. No luck. So he started walking once again.

Seventy miles later he was in Columbia, Tennessee, where he found work with a tailor named James Shelton. Andy did good work, and was known for giving customers a "snug fit." Mrs. Shelton treated Andy like a son. Years later, after he became president, she often said that she had taught Andrew Johnson how to read and write. When asked, the president said, "She did not. But she seemed to get so much pleasure out of saying she did that I have not denied it. I am glad to give her all the pleasure that I can, for she was a mother to me when I lived with them and worked at my trade with her husband."

Columbia was a growing town of about 1,500 people, with many shows, taverns, and churches. Andy could have made a good life for himself there as a tailor. Six months later, however, he heard that things had grown worse for his mother. Andy hurried home to see what he could do.

But Andy could not stay in Raleigh. So he convinced his mother and his stepfather to go with him to Tennessee. Polly's brother Andrew McDonough and several other relatives were living in the Sequatchie Valley of eastern Tennessee. Andy's brother Bill had already gone to live on their farm. Maybe they could all make a fresh start there.

Andy loaded the family's few things onto a two-wheel cart pulled by a blind pony. Another tailor named A. D. February went with them as Andy faced the trip across the mountains one more time.

This trip was even harder than the one before. The horse could not pull all four of them at once. So they used the "ride and tie" method of traveling: Andy and February took turns with Polly and Turner. They would walk for and hour, and then ride for an hour. It was a slow way to travel. Sometimes they only managed 10 or 15 miles a day. They slept out in the open, and cooked their meals over an open fire. One night a panther came and knocked their skillet off the fire. Another night Andy had to chase away a bear with his shotgun.

At last, in September 1826, the tired and dirty travelers came to a hill. Below them lay the town of Greeneville, a beautiful little Scotch-Irish town in the heart of eastern Tennessee.

Andy went into town to find food for the horses and passed a group of young girls. One of them was 16-year-old Eliza McCardle, the only child of a Scottish shoemaker who had died. The story is told that Eliza said to her friends, "There goes my beau, girls, mark it." Some say Johnson told his mother that day that he was going to marry that girl.

But Greeneville had a tailor, so Andy and the others moved on to the town of Rutledge some 40 miles away. For six months he set up shop as a tailor. But he could not forget that pretty brown-haired girl with the large hazel eyes. When at last he heard that the tailor in Greeneville had closed his shop, Andy did not hesitate. In March 1827, he packed up and moved his family back to Greeneville.

Andy visited Eliza often at her widowed mother's house, where she worked with her mother making quilts to earn their living. Their courtship developed quickly. Soon Andy proposed. Eliza said yes at once.

On May 17, 1827, Andrew Johnson and Eliza McCardle were married in the McCardle home by Mordecai Lincoln, a distant cousin of Abraham Lincoln. She was 17, and he was 18. Their marriage would last nearly 50 years.

Years later, William H. Crook, a guard at the White House, said of the Johnsons, "Their temperaments were unlike. He, fervid and aggressive; she calm and retiring—but their union was fortunate, and, by her aid, he was better prepared for the long encounter which fate held in reserve."

Johnson rented a small cottage on Main Street. Over the front door he hung the simple sign, "A. Johnson, Tailor." The house had two rooms—each about 12 feet by 12 feet. In the front room, he set up his tailoring shop. In the back room, he and Eliza made their home.

Eliza McCardle, who married Andrew Johnson at the age of 17 in May 1827.

Eliza had been formally educated at Greeneville's Rhea Academy. She did not teach Andy to read, as some stories have said, for he already knew how. But at the end of each day, by candlelight, she taught him how to write and do arithmetic. Andrew Johnson must have been bursting with the desire to express himself on paper. Even his simple account books were scrawled all over in the margins with practice signatures. He would never be a very good speller. Once, years later, a secretary told him that he had misspelled his own name. Johnson shot back: "It is a man of small imagination who cannot spell his name more than one way."

Those account books showed that Johnson was quickly becoming a successful businessman. At first he was worried about having his own shop. Then John A. Brown placed an order. Johnson made him a coat of heavy cloth with steel buttons. He did such a fine job that another customer ordered a full suit. Soon his reputation for making perfect fitting, stylish clothes spread through the town. He would make a coat for $3.50. A pair of pants cost $1.50. And he charged $10.00 for a full suit. He did expert work and always finished on time as promised. Soon Greeneville's best-dressed citizens were flooding him with orders for new clothes.

Even the children in town sang his praises:

If you want a brand-new coat
I'll tell you what to do:
Go down to Andrew Johnson's shop
And get a long tail blue.

If you want the girls to love you,
To love you good and true,
Go down to Andy's tailor shop
And get a long tail blue.

During the next two years, he and Eliza lived simply and saved every penny they could. Andy had to hire assistants to help him handle all the work. In the back of the little Main Street shop, their first children were born: Martha in 1828, and then Charles in 1830.

Only a few years before, Andy had been a penniless, orphaned, runaway apprentice. Now he had a wonderful family and a growing, respected tailor shop of his own. He had learned to write and could read any book he could lay his hands on. Life seemed almost perfect.

But Andrew Johnson had only begun.

WORKINGMAN'S HERO

"Some day I will show the stuck-up aristocrats
who is running this country. A cheap purse-
proud set they are, not half as good as the man
who earns his bread by the sweat of his brow."

ANDREW JOHNSON

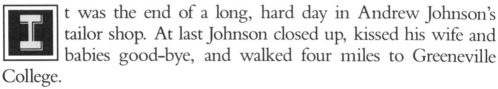

It was the end of a long, hard day in Andrew Johnson's tailor shop. At last Johnson closed up, kissed his wife and babies good-bye, and walked four miles to Greeneville College.

Johnson could never have enrolled in this college, or in nearby Washington or Tusculum Colleges. As a working man, husband, and father, he could not afford the time or the tuition. But every Friday night, Greeneville College's debating society met to argue political and philosophical issues of the day. And Johnson had won permission to join in.

These lively meetings were another major step in his self-designed education. Here he learned to sharpen his passionate, tumbling thoughts into razor-sharp ideas. He learned how to speak in a way that commanded attention. And he learned how to persuade.

The students who came were younger, richer, and formally educated. But they were drawn to Johnson's dark, serious look and slow, controlled voice. They began to stop by his shop during the week. One student wrote: "On approaching the village there stood on the hill by the highway a solitary little house, perhaps ten feet square. We invariably entered when passing. It contained a bed, two or three stools, and a tailor's platform. Here we delighted to stop, because one lived here whom we knew outside of school, and he made us welcome; one who would amuse us by his social good nature, one who took more than ordinary interest in catering to our pleasure."

He and the town plasterer, Blackston McDannel, often disagreed on things. One day McDannel challenged Johnson to a public debate. The subject: Tennessee's legal powers in the state's Cherokee territories. Johnson accepted the challenge.

In an age with no television, radio, or movies, public debates were a popular form of entertainment. People came from miles around to hear the two men speak. McDannel went first and spoke from a long written text. Then it was Johnson's turn. "He hit the nail on the top every pop," said McDannel. The two became fast friends.

Johnson's thirst for knowledge grew. He hired a reader at 50 cents a day to read to him from newspapers, speeches, and books as he worked. Soon his shop became quite a gathering place for working men. Johnson sat on his workbench, continuously stitching. Around him farmers, teachers, and laborers argued local politics—and asked for his opinions.

The time was right for a self-made man like Andrew Johnson.

On March 4, 1829, Andrew Jackson was elected the seventh president of the United States. It was a new era in American politics. The presidents before him—Washington, the Adamses, Jefferson, Madison, and Monroe—had been members of the Eastern educated elite. But Jackson was different. He was a famous Indian fighter who became a hero—"Old Hickory"—at the Battle of New Orleans, a decisive American victory in the War of 1812. The American democracy had elected a frontiersman, a real working man president. Jackson became a symbol for the majority of Americans: the common man who worked with his hands, who owned no property—who owned no slaves.

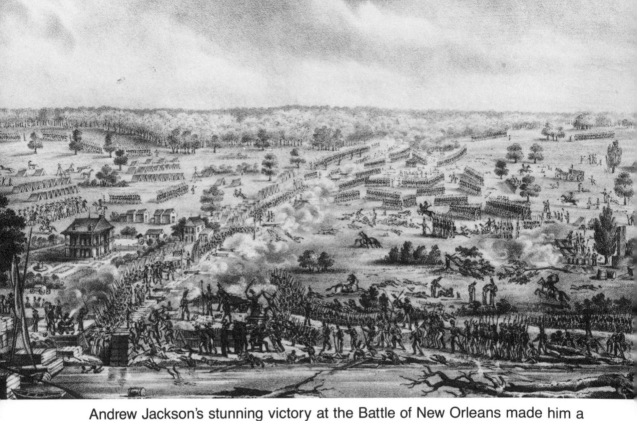

Andrew Jackson's stunning victory at the Battle of New Orleans made him a popular hero. In this engraving, British troops (right) attack the American lines.

Jackson's election was cheered by the working men who gathered in Andrew Johnson's tailor shop. Then they listened to Johnson speak out against the prejudice of the aristocratic ruling class. They heard him say that the aristocrats' money did not buy them the right to rule, that wealth did not equal ability. They heard him proudly claim to be a "plebeian"—an honest working man. And they saw that they had a man much like Jackson right here in Greeneville.

At the time of the next town counsel, several of these young men drew up a slate of working class candidates—"mechanics," as they were called at the time. Among the seven aldermen elected were Blackston McDannel, Mordecai Lincoln—and Andrew Johnson.

Johnson did a fine job. He always spoke out for his common neighbors, and they re-elected him twice. In the spring of 1832, his friends and neighbors did something even more astonishing: They managed to elect him mayor.

Many of the town's wealthy "slaveocracy"—the rich, powerful landowners who owned slaves—were shocked. How could they bear to be represented by a man who earned a living sewing up britches? Twice they would try to get rid of him, but Johnson was always elected to another term. Johnson was hooked. His ambition was ignited. He would spend most of the rest of his life seeking higher public office.

Then Johnson accepted what must have been an even greater honor. The county court appointed the unschooled tailor a trustee of Rhea Academy.

Meanwhile, Johnson's tailoring business continued to grow. And his family had grown too: another daughter, named Mary, and another son, named Robert. At last he and Eliza used some of their savings to realize one of their dreams. They bought a comfortable home on Water Street. "Without a home there can be no good citizen," he said; "with a home there can be no bad one."

Johnson's hard work was finally paying off. He was becoming a well-known, successful citizen of Greeneville. And like many well-to-do people in Tennessee, Johnson now bought several slaves to cook, keep house, and work alongside him his vegetable garden out back. The first one was a young girl named Dolly, whom he bought for $500. Later Johnson bought her half-brother, Sam, who was known for imitating his owner by wearing a top hat and a black silk coat to church on Sunday. Altogether, Johnson would own eight or nine slaves, though it is said that he never sold any.

In the spring of 1835, the newly successful Johnson set his sights even higher. At the age of 26, he decided to run for the Tennessee state legislature. He was eager to debate his opponents, Major Matthew Stephenson and Major James Britton. Johnson's debating style was sharp and aggressive. He blasted his wealthy Whig opponents with personal attacks. He amazed the audience with endless hard, cold facts. Britton dropped out of the race entirely.

When election day came, Johnson soundly beat Stephenson by 1,413 votes to 800. Johnson leased out his tailor shop and headed for the Tennessee capital of Nashville, a town between 5,000 and 6,000 residents.

Johnson arrived in Nashville in early October and took his seat in the legislature quietly. He studied the rules, he watched the more experienced speakers, and he got to know his surroundings. When he felt sure of himself, he would speak.

Johnson was 5 feet 10, tall for the time. He dressed in black, which emphasized his dark hair, smooth dark complexion, and intense black eyes. One observer wrote: "Though plainly clad and not so robust in figure as in later life, his marked and expressive features presented him well and engaged attention when he rose to speak. He made more than the ordinary impression of a new member. He was punctual, laborious, but not unduly forward." He had an honest, direct style of making his point in "a clear and mellow voice."

But Johnson was inexperienced. He believed in many lofty ideals. He supported the common working man and was against wasteful government spending. But he did not yet know how to mesh such grand principles with the practical "real-world" laws on which he had to vote.

He voted against granting a charter to bring the Hiawassee Railroad into Tennessee. "A railroad!" he exclaimed. "Why, it would frighten horses, put the owners of public vehicles out of business, break up inns and taverns and be a monopoly generally."

Although Eliza was raising the children as Methodists, Johnson refused to join any particular church. When a bill was proposed to open each session of the legislature with a prayer, Johnson was against it. The United States Constitution guaranteed separation of church and state. Johnson felt the legislators should go to church if they needed some religious instruction.

Then Johnson voted against government spending to improve state roads. He said it was a waste of money.

Unfortunately, the people back home favored trains, prayers, and better roads. Especially the roads. Western and middle Tennessee had many fine waterways, making commercial travel easy. Eastern Tennessee was rough, mountainous countryside that made travel difficult—and the voters desperately wanted the government to build better roads.

Johnson had voted his conscience. But he had not listened to the voters. When he ran for re-election in 1837, the voters instead sent him back to his tailor shop.

Johnson did not let this lesson go unheeded. Home again, he thought through the mistakes he had made. For the next two years, he spent as much time as a working tailor could with the people of Greeneville. He was not a joker or a gossip, but he was good at talking about ideas and listening. And he had become too ambitious to give up on politics.

When he ran for the state house again in 1839, he won. In 1841, the voters sent him to the state senate.

Johnson had won over the common people of Eastern Tennessee. Now in the senate he made enemies out of the state's "slaveocracy." Population figures in an area were used for deciding how many representatives that area had in the legislature. Each slave counted as three-fifths of a man. This gave powerful slave owners an advantage. Johnson believed this rule was unfair to east Tennesseans, who owned few slaves. He tried to get it removed from the state constitution, but the rich landowners fought him and won.

And they targeted Andrew Johnson as an enemy.

WASHINGTON

"I am a mechanic, and when a blow is struck on
that class I will resent it."

JOHNSON, RESPONDING IN A SENATE DEBATE
TO A SLUR ON THE WORKING CLASS

A ndrew Johnson had been born poor and powerless in North Carolina. He built a business and a political career in the mountains of Tennessee, where he had become a champion of the common working man. Now he was taking those ideas—and his ambition—to Washington.

In the fall of 1843, Johnson rode on horseback into the rowdy half-built town of Washington, D.C. The 34 year-old ex-tailor was going to sit down with some of the most powerful men in the nation. For Andrew Johnson had been elected to the U.S. House of Representatives.

He found a room at Mrs. Russell's boardinghouse on North Capitol Street. From there he would be able to visit his daughter Martha, who was attending Georgetown Female Seminary. But Washington was not Andy Johnson's style. He did not go in for the theater and parties and the many social gatherings. Besides, who had time when there were so many books at the Library of Congress just waiting to be read?

Johnson was elected as a Democrat, but he soon proved himself to be an independent thinker. Sometimes his convictions led him to vote with other Southern congressmen. Slavery was becoming a divisive issue in Congress. Many people in the North, called abolitionists, wanted the U.S. government to abolish—or end—slavery completely, with no financial compensation to the Southern slave owner. Southern states believed that each individual state had a right to decide for itself whether to allow slavery. Johnson joined other southern politicians in defending slavery as a necessary part of the nation's agricultural economy.

But he split with most Southerners over another growing issue. Northerners supported a strong federal government. Southerners believed in states' rights. They believed that the nation was a collection of individual states, and that each state had a right to take care of its own business within its own state borders. Here Johnson disagreed. Though he believed in the rights of each state, nothing was more important to him than the Union as a whole and the Constitution.

Another issue was the westward expansion of the United States. Settlers were moving into huge untamed lands in the western territories, lands that were owned by the federal government. Johnson proposed a new law called the Homestead Act, "A Bill to authorize every poor man in the United States who is the head of a family, to enter one hundred and sixty acres of the public domain, 'without money and without price.' " He believed this would help the nation by encouraging eager, hard-working people to settle the region. And it would give the common folk a chance to own land and homes. The bill did not become law, but Johnson would never give up fighting to get it passed. He would reintroduce the bill at every session as long as he remained a member of Congress.

Johnson quickly became known as the Mechanic Statesman, since he had been one of the people who worked with the hands—tailors, carpenters, blacksmiths, craftsmen. Once a fellow congressman seemed to insult his poor background. Johnson responded with anger and pride: "Sir, I do not forget that I am a mechanic. I am proud to own it. Neither do I forget that Adam was a tailor and sewed fig leaves, or that our Saviour was the son of a carpenter."

Johnson spoke his mind, and often suffered the consequences. Back home in Tennessee, members of the conservative Whig party had had enough of Johnson's independent politics. They knew they could not defeat this popular "man of the people" at the polls. So since the Whigs had a majority in the state legislature, they found another way. They changed the boundaries of the congressional districts. Now Johnson's district had more Whigs than Democrats. In 1852, after 10 years of service in the House of Representatives, Johnson was defeated. "Fellow citizens," he told some of this constituents, "the Whigs have cheated me out of Congress, they have torn the county of Greene from its sister counties, and attached it to a lot of foreign counties. They have split it up till it looks like a salamander. The fact is they have 'gerrymandered' me out of Congress."

Andy Johnson said good-bye to Washington—for now. But there was no way he was going to say good-bye to politics.

"MECHANIC" GOVERNOR OF TENNESSEE

"You have underestimated my opponent. I have
never met so powerful a speaker as Andrew
Johnson."

MAJOR GUSTAVUS HENRY, JOHNSON'S OPPONENT IN
THE RACE FOR GOVERNOR OF TENNESSEE

ustavus A. Henry was a well-known lawyer in Tennessee. He was a descendant of the Revolution's Patrick Henry, famous for the oath "Give me liberty, or give me death!" Gustavus Henry was a famous speaker, too, and was known as the "Eagle Orator."

Johnson picked a tough fight when he decided to run against Henry for governor of Tennessee.

Johnson and Henry met head-on as they "stumped" across the state making speeches and debating the issues. In one debate, Henry tried to make Johnson look bad. "When in Congress," Henry said, "my honorable opponent voted against a resolution to appropriate money for famine-stricken Ireland. How could any one be so inhuman, so heartless, as to cast such a vote?"

Johnson answered easily that the charge was true. He had voted against using the poor man's tax dollar for that cause. "But that is not all of the story," he added. "For when I voted against that resolution, I turned to my fellow Congressmen and proposed to give fifty dollars of my own funds if they would give a like amount, and when they declined the proposition, I ran my hand in my pocket, Major Henry, and pulled out fifty dollars of good money, which I donated to the cause. How much did you give, sir?"

Johnson won the election. On October 3, 1853, he became Tennessee's "Mechanic Governor."

From the governor's chair, Johnson continued to fight for the common man. He never forgot his deprived childhood—how his eager young mind had been locked out of school for the lack of a few dollars. In his first term of office, the self-educated governor worked to improve educational opportunities. "All who entertain any personal and state pride," he said, "must feel deeply wounded... that Tennessee, though fifth state in the Union, stands lowest in the list of education, save one.... While millions are appropriated to aid in the various works of internal improvements, can there be nothing done for education?" Johnson oversaw the creation of the first free public school in Tennessee. He established a free public library so that anyone, no matter how poor, could have access to books—and the world's greatest ideas.

When Johnson was up for re-election two years later, he was challenged by Meredith P. Gentry of a party known as the "Know-Nothings." During nearly three months of campaigning, the two men debated nearly 60 times.

"Alas, my fellow countrymen," said Gentry, "The State of Tennessee does not need prayers; there is a curse resting on her—and first that curse must be removed. I have come forth from my retirement and my prayers are joined with yours to remove that curse—and that curse is Andrew Johnson."

The Know-Nothings were against allowing foreigners and Catholics to hold political power. They got their nickname from the fact that they were a secret, unofficial political party, and when members were questioned about their beliefs they were told to respond, "I know nothing." Though Johnson did not belong to any particular church, he strongly believed that religious bigotry and hatred of foreigners was completely against the Constitution. He charged that the Know-Nothings were no better than a band of outlaws. "Show me a Know-Nothing," exclaimed Johnson, "and I will show you a loathsome reptile, on whose neck every honest man should set his feet." Even some Democrats asked Johnson to tone down his speeches. He must stop defending foreigners and Catholics. After all, his supporters were all Protestant. "Gentlemen," Johnson told them, "I will make that same speech tomorrow if it blows the Democratic party to hell."

Gentry charged that Johnson was not really a Southern man—that in Congress he had sided too often with Yankees. His supporters made fun of Johnson's poor background, and called him "low, despicable and dirty."

Johnson's response grew bolder and more sure: "Whose hands built your Capitol? Whose toil, whose labor built your railroads and your ships? Does not all life rest on labor?... There are in Congress two hundred and twenty-three Congressmen, and of this large number all are lawyers except twenty-three. The laboring man of America is ignored.... For my part, I say let the mechanic and the laborer make our laws, rather than the idle and vicious aristocrat."

Johnson was easily re-elected. He continued to work for a better educational system. He started regular state fairs to encourage interest and support of the small, independent farmer.

The Democrats now controlled the state legislature. On October 8, 1857, they voted to elect Johnson to be a United States senator from Tennessee.

Once again, Andy Johnson packed up and headed for Washington, D.C. He later told fellow senators, "I have reached the summit of my ambition. The acme of all my hopes has been attained, and I would not give the position I occupy today for any other in the United States."

Johnson had no way of knowing the important positions he had yet to fill.

7

"I AM A UNION MAN!"

"When the crisis comes, I will be found standing
by the Union."

ANDREW JOHNSON, SPEAKING TO A FRIEND
THE DAY BEFORE THE 1860 ELECTION

By now, the late autumn leaves along the roads from Tennessee to Washington, D.C., were a familiar sight to Andrew Johnson. He had traveled these highways as representative for Tennessee over four terms, a total of eight years. Now, after two terms as governor, he was returning to Washington as a United States senator. He was a few weeks short of being 50 years old.

Johnson walked from his rooms at the St. Charles Hotel to his swearing-in ceremony on December 7, 1857. All around him sat the sons of some of the nation's oldest, wealthiest landed families—the finest gentlemen, who had studied at the country's best colleges and universities. The ambitious, self-taught Johnson never questioned his right to be there representing the common people of Tennessee. But he would never lose his prejudice against the privileged aristocracy.

Seated near him was fellow Southerner Jefferson Davis—a senator from Mississippi who would later serve as president of the Confederacy. Davis later said of Johnson:

The position of Mr. Johnson with his associates of the South had never been pleasant, not from any fault…on their side, but solely due to the intense…sensitive pride of Mr. Johnson….Mr. Johnson seemed to set before his mind…his democratic or plebeian origin as a bar to warm social relations. This pride—for it was the pride of having no pride—his associates long struggled to overcome. They respected Mr. Johnson's ability, integrity and great original force of character, but nothing could make him be, or seem to wish to feel, at home in their society. Some casual word in debate would seem to wound him to the quick…." But Davis added, "His habits were marked by temperance, industry, courage and unswerving perseverance.

One of Johnson's first acts as United States senator was to introduce the Homestead Act. "I can go back to that period in my history when I could not say that I had a home," he told his fellow senators. "This being so, when I cast my eyes over one extreme of the United States to the other, and behold the great numbers that are homeless, I feel for them… Transfer the man from the point where he is producing nothing…In a short time he has a crop…He becomes a better man for all government purpose, because he is interested in the country in which he lives."

But Andrew Johnson's concern for the "common people" was about to put him at the center of a controversy that had been building pressure like steam in a boiler since the United States' very beginning more than 70 years before. Now this controversy was about to explode. The issue was slavery.

West of Tennessee and the Mississippi River, the United States was still largely a wilderness. Few Americans lived there. Government there was still in its infancy—much of the area was still organized into "territories" that had not yet become official states of the Union.

Johnson's Homestead Act was a plan that would help bring the territories of the vast American West into the union of American states, the United States.

On the face of it, the Homestead Act seemed like a good idea. It would give average Americans a chance to own land and homes without having to come up with large sums of money. And it would help the United States as a whole by speeding up the settlement and productive use of the West.

But the Southern states in the East were against the Homestead Act. This was not because the act helped ordinary people get homes. Nor was it because these states were against the development of the West. The Southern states were against the Homestead Act because of what would happen afterwards.

The people who went west as a result of the Homestead Act would not be large plantation operators. Their economy would not depend on slave labor. The West would be populated by small farmers. When the Western states entered the Union, they would enter as "free" or "non-slave" states, giving the Northern, industrialized states more votes on their side of the slavery issue.

By defending the interests of the common man—and by always taking an independent path—Andrew Johnson earned the hatred of many of his fellow Southerners. Yet Johnson did not agree with Northern senators who believed slavery should be completely abolished, or ended.

Now many Southerners began to talk of their right to secede— to leave the Union. The states had joined the Union voluntarily— but Southerners believed their states had remained individuals, with the right to manage much of their own affairs within their own borders. If they no longer agreed with the way the way that nation was being run, they had a right to withdraw their "membership." But most Northerners believed in a strong federal government and a Union that was more important than any individual state. A state could not just split because it disagreed with this law or that.

Tensions grew in Washington as the 1860 presidential election approached. A new political party in the North called the Republican party nominated Abraham Lincoln, a country lawyer from Illinois, who was against expansion of slavery in the West. Johnson's own party, the Democrats nominated John C. Breckinridge of Kentucky.

On November 6, 1860, Abraham Lincoln was elected the 16th president of the United States. For many Southerners, this was the last straw. South Carolinians met to discuss secession. Many people wondered: What would happen? Had secession been a lot of talk— like a kid threatening to go home if the others refuse to play his way? Or would Southerners really break away from the Union?

In December, spectators filled the galleries of the Unites States Senate to listen as, one by one, Northern and Southern politicians argued and shouted over what should be done. On December 18, they sat breathlessly as Southern Senator Andrew Johnson boldly declared his feelings: "I am opposed to Secession," he said. "No state has the right to secede from this Union without the consent of the other states... If the doctrine of Secession is to be carried out upon the mere whim of a state this government is at an end..."

"What then is the issue?" he demanded of his fellow Southerners. "It is this and only this, we are mad because Mr. Lincoln has been elected President and we have not got our man. If we had got our man we should not be for breaking up the Union, but as Mr. Lincoln was elected we are for breaking up the Union! I say, no, let us show ourselves men and men of courage.... Though I fought against Lincoln I love my country; I love the Constitution... Senators, my blood, my existence, I would give to save the Union."

Both Northerners and Southerners were stunned by the bold speech. Northerners stood up and cheered him as a hero right there on the Senate floor. Southern senators hissed insults at him or refused even to look at him as he left the Senate chamber.

The *New York Herald* said Johnson's speech was "the talk of every circle in Washington and was uniformly condemned by southern men." The *Chicago Tribune* wrote that Johnson had the "honor of striking the first really stunning blow at the treason of the seceding States." Jefferson Davis called him "the southern traitor." Johnson's reply was: "I say to every Senator... to every man that loves his country... if you are for preserving this Union in its great and fundamental principles, I am your ally, without reference to your antecedents or what may take place hereafter." Copies of the speech

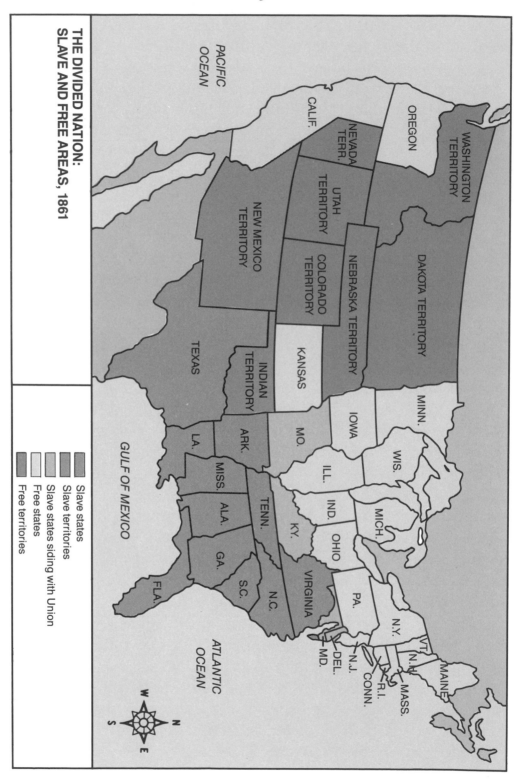

THE DIVIDED NATION:
SLAVE AND FREE AREAS, 1861

Slave states
Slave territories
Slave states siding with Union
Free states
Free territories

were in great demand, and people throughout the county sent telegrams and letters filled with praise, insults, and even death threats to the independent-minded Southern senator. Senator Clingman from North Carolina later declared that Johnson's speech was what had finally brought on the Civil War.

As others around him took sides in the growing split, Johnson stood quite alone. Of all the Southern senators, Johnson was the only one to declare himself for the Union.

Two days later, on December 20, 1860, the Southern state of South Carolina became the first state to secede from the Union. Delegates meeting in Charleston declared, "The union now subsisting between South Carolina and other States, under the name of 'The United States of America,' is hereby dissolved." With this action they told the rest of the nation—and the world—that newly elected President Abraham Lincoln would have no power within their borders.

During the next two months, other Southern states joined South Carolina: Mississippi, Florida, Alabama, Georgia, Louisiana, and Texas. No one was quite sure where this would all lead. In February, delegates from the seceded Southern states met in Montgomery, Alabama, and formed the Confederate States of America. Johnson's colleague, Jefferson Davis, was elected president of the new nation. Through it all, Johnson was steadfast in his support of the Constitution and the Union. In March, Johnson gave another stirring, patriotic speech, in which he quoted the "Star-Spangled Banner" and called the Southerners "traitors." And he added, Were I the President of the United States...I would have them arrested, and if convicted...by the eternal God, I would execute them!" Again the Senate rang with cheers and applause. The next day the *New York Times* said, "His name is in every mouth today, and he is freely applauded as the greatest man of the age."

In his inaugural speech on March 4, President Lincoln declared the nation "unbroken." Southerners had no reason to fear his administration, he said. "I have no purpose directly or indirectly to interfere with the institution of slavery. I believe I have no lawful right to do so and I have no inclination to do so." What happened now depended on what *Southerners* chose to do. "In *your* hands, my dissatisfied fellow-countrymen, and not in *mine*, is the momentous issue of civil war. The government will not assail [attack] *you*. You can have no conflict, without being yourselves the aggressor."

Few people believed at this point that the conflict would actually lead to war. But Lincoln had sworn to protect all federal property in Southern states, including Fort Sumter, which was on a small island off the coast of South Carolina. Lincoln let it be known he was sending in supplies. The Confederates, however, could not bear to see the Stars and Stripes—now a "foreign" flag—flying over such an important Southern port. On April 12, Confederate general P. G. T. Beauregard began to fire on the fort. Thirty-four hours later, Union major Robert Anderson surrendered the fort to the Confederates.

No one was killed during the battle. But the shots rang out a clear message: The Civil War had begun.

At the end of the Senate session, Johnson left Washington for home. He hoped to help persuade Tennesseans to stay with the Union. Tennessee was one of the "border states." These states were geographically—and politically—between the North and the Deep South. The people's feelings were often mixed, and varied from one town to the next.

Johnson's trip home, however, was rocky. Everywhere emotions were running high. In Liberty, Virginia, an armed mob rushed into Johnson's train.

"Are you Andy Johnson?" one man shouted in his face.

"I am," said Johnson.

"Then I am Going to pull your nose!" The man reached forward, but Johnson drew out his pistol. Women screamed as the crowd backed out, trying to drag Johnson with them. As the train pulled away from the station, the crowd continued to shout insults at him—but Johnson shouted in return: "I am a Union man!"

Throughout the South, angry Southerners were hanging Johnson in effigy. In Lynchburg, Virginia, a mob succeeded in dragging him from the train. They beat him and spat on him, and even wrapped a noose around his neck and almost hanged him. But someone shouted, "His neighbors in Greenville have made arrangements to hang their Senator on his arrival. Virginians have no right to deprive them of that privilege."

Even in Tennessee, Johnson met with jeers and shouts of "Traitor!" Still he traveled the mountain roads of eastern Tennessee, talking with his friends and neighbors, trying to convince them to stand with the Union. But the tide of rebellion was too strong. On May 7, the Tennessee legislature formed a military alliance with the confederate government. Three more states—Arkansas, North Carolina, and Virginia—seceded. In June, the people of Tennessee went to the polls to decide on the issue of secession. The final vote: 104,914 for secession, only 47,328 against. Tennessee became the 11th state to join the Confederacy.

Once again Andy Johnson was forced to leave his home. Only this time—branded a traitor by his fellow Tennesseeans—he fled for his life. Eight years would pass before he would once again walk the streets of Greeneville.

8

A HERO AND A TRAITOR

"We have commenced the battle of freedom. . . . I
say, let the battle go on—until the Stars and
Stripes shall again be unfurled upon every cross-
road, and from every housetop."
ANDREW JOHNSON, SPEAKING ON THE SENATE FLOOR
SHORTLY AFTER THE START OF THE CIVIL WAR

ennesseeans called Johnson a traitor and chased him from the South. But Northerners welcomed him with open arms and called him a hero.

Northern confidence was high. President Lincoln had called for 75,000 troops to put down the rebellion. Most people in the North thought the whole matter could be settled within a few months at the most.

Then, in July 1861, Union and Confederate troops met for the first time near Manassas, Virginia, near a little stream called Bull Run. Everyone knew in advance that the battle would take place. Finely dressed ladies and gentlemen drove out from Washington, their buggies loaded with fried chicken, biscuits, cakes, and pies. It was a fine day to spread out a picnic and watch the Union soldiers put Johnny Reb in his place.

But the battle was far from a sporting event. Two unprepared, untrained, loosely formed armies battled in the heat and dust and confusion. Before the day was over, the picnickers and troops were fleeing back to Washington, screaming that the Rebels were at their heels.

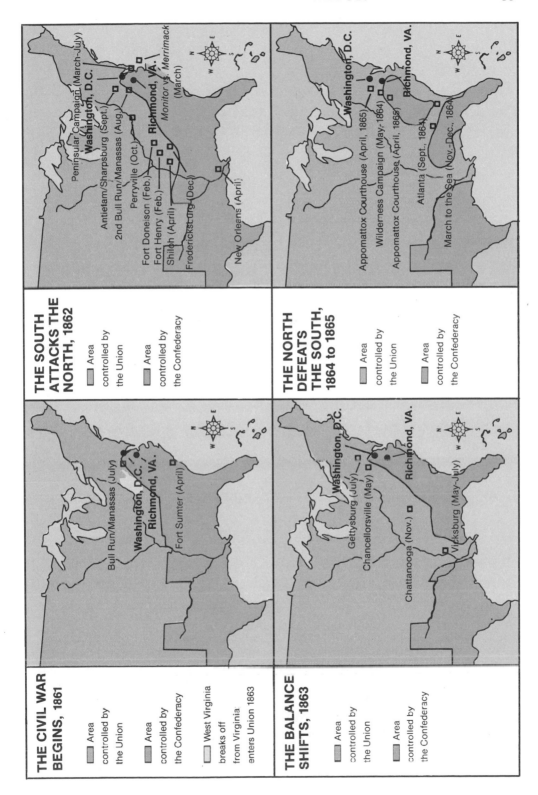

THE CIVIL WAR BEGINS, 1861

■ Area controlled by the Union

■ Area controlled by the Confederacy

■ West Virginia breaks off from Virginia enters Union 1863

Bull Run/Manassas (July)

Washington, D.C.

Richmond, VA.

Fort Sumter (April)

THE SOUTH ATTACKS THE NORTH, 1862

■ Area controlled by the Union

■ Area controlled by the Confederacy

Peninsular Campaign (March-July)

Washington, D.C.

Richmond, VA.

Monitor vs. Merrimack (March)

Antietam/Sharpsburg (Sept.)

2nd Bull Run/Manassas (Aug.)

Perryville (Oct.)

Fort Donelson (Feb.)

Fort Henry (Feb.)

Shiloh (April)

Fredericksburg (Dec.)

New Orleans (April)

THE BALANCE SHIFTS, 1863

■ Area controlled by the Union

■ Area controlled by the Confederacy

Washington, D.C.

Richmond, VA.

Gettysburg (July)

Chancellorsville (May)

Chattanooga (Nov.)

Vicksburg (May-July)

THE NORTH DEFEATS THE SOUTH, 1864 to 1865

■ Area controlled by the Union

■ Area controlled by the Confederacy

Washington, D.C.

Richmond, VA.

Appomattox Courthouse (April, 1865)

Wilderness Campaign (May-1864)

Appomattox Courthouse (April, 1865)

Atlanta (Sept. 1864)

March to the Sea Nov.-Dec., 1864

The North was stunned. As wounded soldiers were brought into Washington, people saw for the first time that perhaps this was going to be a real war after all.

The news from Tennessee that summer and fall was bad. Though the state as a whole had seceded, many of the people of eastern Tennessee remained loyal to the Union—for which the people suffered. They were turned out of their homes, harassed, put in prison, and sometimes even hanged. Johnson's own family was turned out of their Greeneville home so it could be used for a Confederate barracks. Johnson begged Lincoln to intervene and recapture the state, and he was frustrated by the failure of Union generals to act. "My own family has been turned into the streets and my house has been turned into barracks and for what?" Johnson bellowed to the Senate. "Because I stood by the Constitution. This is my offense."

At last, Union general Ulysses S. Grant captured Fort Henry and Fort Donelson and invaded western and central Tennessee. But Johnson's home of eastern Tennessee remained in the hands of the Confederates.

Johnson's loyalty had not escaped Lincoln's notice. In March 1862, he appointed Johnson military governor of Tennessee. His job would be to use military powers to restore order and form a temporary government until a loyal government could be formed.

As the elected governor of Tennessee years before, Johnson had been chosen by the people to run the state. His appointment as military governor met with approval throughout the Union. But his arrival in the capital of Nashville was not greeted with enthusiasm, for the people in the town—and much of the state—were still predominantly for secession.

Johnson faced the opposition with his commitment to the Union and his speechmaking skills. The first order of business for the military governor was to win back the capitol itself. General D. C. Buell's troops had recaptured the city militarily, but not the citizens' loyalty. In his first speech, in front of the St. Cloud Hotel, Johnson told a crowd, "I come with the olive branch in one hand and the Constitution in the other to render you whatever aid may be in my power in re-erecting... the Star Spangled Banner." A few days later, Johnson cleared out the entire pro-Confederate Nashville city government when he demanded that all officeholders take an oath of loyalty to the Union. He took over the bank and closed down Confederate newspapers.

As military governor of Tennessee, Johnson had the rank of brigadier general in the Union army. From the beginning, he had many disagreements with the way General Buell was handling the army in Tennessee. He complained to Lincoln and to the war department several times. In a letter to Lincoln he wrote that the general was doing such a terrible job of defending Tennessee that "General Buell is very popular with the Rebels."

All summer long, the Confederate armies advanced. In early August, Johnson got reports that Confederate general Nathan B. Forrest was within six miles of Nashville. On August 10, there was not doubt that the Confederates were within striking distance of the capital. All communications between Nashville and Washington were severed. Barely two weeks later, Confederate troops captured the town of Gallatin, Tennessee. Gallatin was an important station along the Louisville-Nashville Railroad that supplied Nashville with food and other supplies. A reporter noted, "The coolness and calmness of the Governor amid these trying scenes are beyond all praise."

Johnson was furious, however, because he believed General Buell did not consider Nashville very important and was prepared to give it up.

For the time being, the Confederates had the upper hand in Kentucky. From here, General Braxton Bragg drove north into Tennessee. He went around Buell's Union troops, then outran them and captured 4,000 troops at Munfordville. The way things were going, Johnson's low opinion of General Buell seemed justified.

Then the Confederate advance lost its energy. Generals who were supposed to meet and combine troops did not. Bragg's invasion came to an end in Perryville, Kentucky, where both armies seemed confused and blundering. The battle of Perryville

Union general Don Carlos Buell, fourth from right, angered Johnson by his conduct of the war in Tennessee.

occurred when Union and Confederate troops ran into each other unexpectedly—General Buell did not even know there was a fight on until it was almost over. Before either side had won any advantage, Bragg withdrew the Confederates. Meanwhile, Buell stood by and let them go. A few weeks later, the war department called General Buell back to Washington. To Andrew Johnson's relief, he was replaced by a brave, well-liked commander named William S. Rosecrans, known to his friends as "Old Rosy."

It was the battle of Murfreesboro that finally sent Bragg's Confederates retreating back into Kentucky. Rosecrans's troops marched south and met them on the morning of New Year's Eve. By nightfall, the Confederates seemed to have the advantage. Then, for nearly three days, both armies faced each other in a standoff—inactive most of time. Unpredictable as ever, Bragg ordered a retreat on the night of January 3, 1863, and the Union army advanced into Murfreesboro the next day. It was hard to say who, if anyone, had won.

Bragg's troops were just across the border, but for the most part, the Union had control of Tennessee once again. Johnson used the opportunity to travel outside the state again, giving pro-Union speeches throughout Ohio, Pennsylvania, New York, and New Jersey.

Early that spring, Lincoln sent a private message to Johnson, asking him to raise 50,000 black troops to fight for the North. Oddly, Lincoln suggested that Johnson was especially qualified to recruit blacks because he had owned slaves. That summer, Johnson formed two brigades of volunteers and turned them over to Rosecrans.

In the last days of summer, when the peculiar odor of skunkweed carried through the mountains, Confederate troops under General Braxton Bragg marched north through the forests of northwestern Georgia. They were headed for the small town of Chickamauga, just 20 miles south of Chattanooga, Tennessee. Thousands of Union troops were camped along Chickamauga Creek, which ran through town. General George Thomas and General Rosecrans waited in the small frame farmhouses they occupied for headquarters.

Bragg's troops would not attack alone. From the east, Virginians under General James Longstreet were on their way to assist them. From the west, Kentucky troops would be arriving under Bishop Leonidas Polk. Polk had started a career as a military officer, but had left to become a bishop in the Episcopal Church. He rejoined the military when war broke out. On the night of September 18, the hills around Chickamauga were crowded with men. Bragg hoped to push the Yankees into a box canyon. The next morning, they attacked.

The fighting lasted all day. One Confederate remembered, "the dead were piled upon each other...like cord wood, to make passage for advancing columns. The sluggish...Chickamauga ran red with human blood." By nightfall, the Union troops were shaken, but they still held the town.

The next morning at nine o'clock, the Confederates charged again. Bishop Polk attacked General Thomas's men on the eastern, right flank. Longstreet's men attacked on the western, left flank. Bragg's men charged up the middle. When the fighting ended that afternoon, nearly 40,000 men—half Confederates and half Union soldiers—lay dead or dying in the streets. The Confederates held Chickamauga.

Polk, Longstreet, and Thomas knew they had won an important victory. With the Union army on the run, they urged Bragg to push on a few more miles and recapture Chattanooga.

But standing in the town surrounded by the mass of dead soldiers, Bragg did not believe they had the strength to go on—his troops needed time to recover.

The other generals were outraged. He was letting the enemy escape.

Lt. General Ulysses S. Grant became leader of the Union forces in the Civil War.

The confederates had stopped before entering Tennessee, but Johnson and the Union had good reason to worry. From Chickamauga, the Confederates could walk to the border in an hour. A few miles beyond that, if they captured Chattanooga, all of middle Tennessee, including Nashville, would lie exposed.

Bragg's men guarded positions along Missionary Ridge and Lookout Mountain across the Tennessee River from Chattanooga. They waited while the Union's food supplies dwindled. Without help, an entire Union army would be captured or starve to death.

Help came in the form of General Ulysses S. Grant. Given command in the West, he began moving troops from the east and west toward Chattanooga. They seized Brown's Ferry a few miles downstream and managed to get supplies into the city from there. A month later, they took Orchard Knob, a hill neighboring Lookout Mountain. The next day, they took Lookout Mountain itself and forced Bragg's army into a confused retreat. The Confederacy would never again march troops through Tennessee.

With Lincoln's approval, Johnson was already busy organizing statewide elections to restore government under the Union in Tennessee. Then, on June 25, 1864, Johnson received news that he might be returning to Washington again very soon. As expected, the National Union Party (as the Republicans called themselves in this election) nominated Lincoln for a second term as president.

When they asked Lincoln whom he would like as his running mate, he did not hesitate: "Governor Johnson of Tennessee."

VICE-PRESIDENT

"What will the aristocrats do with a rail-splitter
for President and a tailor for Vice-president?"
ANDREW JOHNSON, JOKING, ON LEARNING THAT THE
NATIONAL UNION PARTY CONVENTION HAD CHOSEN
HIM TO BE LINCOLN'S RUNNING MATE

Lincoln's choice of Johnson as a running mate was a political move. He believed it would strengthen the ticket to run with a Southerner from a border state who had remained loyal to the Union. Not everyone was pleased. Thaddeus Stevens grumbled, "Can't you get a candidate for Vice-President without going down into a damned rebel province for one?" The Democrats chose General George B. McClellan to run against Lincoln. McClellan charged that the war had gone on too long. He proposed to end the bloodshed by negotiating a peace with the Confederates.

Just before the election, however, the Union won a major victory. General William T. Sherman ended his "march to the sea" across Georgia by capturing the major city of Atlanta. Morale in the North soared—the war could be won!

On November 8, 1864, Abraham Lincoln was re-elected president, and Andrew Johnson was elected vice-president.

Johnson spent the winter finishing his work in Tennessee. By March, Johnson was in poor health, and was in even worse condition following a long train ride to Washington for the

A Republican campaign poster for the 1864 presidential election.

inauguration. The night before the ceremonies, he spent with a friend, celebrating the inauguration over several whiskies.

The next morning, it was dark and rainy. Johnson took a carriage to the Capitol, with retiring vice-president Hannibal Hamlin. Tired, in poor health, and suffering from a hangover, Johnson did not look well. He may also have been a bit nervous about being sworn in as the vice-president. At last they reached the Capitol and waited to go into the Senate chamber, where Johnson would be sworn in. In the damp, poorly ventilated waiting room, Johnson began to feel nauseated. "Mr. Hamlin," he said at one point, "I am not well and need a stimulant, have you any whiskey?" Hamlin did not, but he sent a page to bring a flask. When it arrived, Johnson drank it and seemed steadier. Then, just before going in, Johnson nervously downed another drink. Then he unsteadily entered the hot, crowded chamber, leaning on Hamlin's arm.

Hamlin gave a farewell speech, which was interrupted several times by latecomers. When Mrs. Lincoln came in, escorted by two senators, the room filled with chatter about the first lady's black velvet outfit. Hamlin finished above the noise as more dignitaries followed.

At last it was Johnson's turn. He stood and began to speak. But this time his words did not come out powerful and strong. He slurred his words. Those in the audience began to look at one another in confusion. After five minutes, Lincoln entered the chamber and sat down. But Johnson continued to speak even over the chatter. He was supposed to speak for only a few minutes, but Johnson rambled on and on. After 15 minutes, it became clear that the new vice-president was drunk. The audience was shocked. One senator covered his face with his hands and laid his head down on his desk. Others chuckled or flushed in outrage. Reporters, sensing a scandal, scribbled away in their notepads

Then it was time for the vice-president to take the oath of office. Instead of placing his hand on the Bible, he took it and held it up. Then he said loudly, "I kiss this Book in the face of my nation of the

United States." The audience was horrified as Johnson was at last hustled from the podium.

The *New York Herald* called the scene "disgraceful in the extreme." The Confederate *Richmond Sentinel* called Johnson a "low sot." Supportive papers, such as the *New York Times*, did not even mention Johnson's drunken behavior. But others called for his resignation.

By contrast, Lincoln's inauguration outside the Capitol was dignified and well praised. The words he spoke became some of the best-remembered words of American history: "With malice toward none, with charity for all, with firmness in the right as God gives us to see the right, let us strive on to finish the work we are in, to bind up the nation's wounds, to care for him who shall have borne the battle and for his widow and his orphan, to do all which may achieve and cherish a just and lasting peace among ourselves and with all nations."

Though there were calls for Johnson, he was not allowed to speak.

Though Lincoln must have been embarrassed by his new vice-president's behavior on such an important day, later he said, "Oh, well, don't you bother about Andy Johnson's drinking. He made a bad slip the other day, but I have known Andy a great many years, and he ain't no drunkard."

But the embarrassing damage to Johnson's reputation had been done.

"And to think," reported the *New York World*, "that one frail life stands between this insolent, clownish creature and the presidency! May God bless and spare Abraham Lincoln!"

The reporters could not have guessed how tragically timely their words were.

FORTY-ONE DAYS

"They shall suffer for this. They shall suffer for this."

ANDREW JOHNSON, PACING HIS ROOMS AFTER SEEING
LINCOLN ON HIS DEATHBED

W hile Johnson quietly suffered through his humiliating start as vice-president, another man known for his hard drinking was dealing the final crushing blows to the South. General Ulysses S. Grant had decided that the only way to defeat the Confederate army was to continue attacking without relief. Near Petersburg, Virginia, only a few miles from the Confederate capital of Richmond, general Robert E. Lee fought on with his tattered, starving army. Lee, like Johnson, was a Southerner from a border state. His father, "Light-horse Harry" Lee, was a hero in the American War of Independence, and Robert E. Lee had spent his whole career in the United States Army. But Lee had stronger family ties to his home state of Virginia and had reluctantly followed its people to join the Confederacy.

At last the Confederates could no longer hold out. They retreated south. Confederate president Jefferson Davis and his government fled from Richmond, and on April 3, 1865, the Confederate capital fell to the Union.

The news sent people shouting and celebrating into the streets of Washington. Johnson was spotted, and the cheering crowd called

For these Union troops at the siege of Petersburg, long stretches of boredom were punctuated by sudden violence.

for a speech. His old self again, Johnson delivered a fiery speech demanding that the leaders of the Confederacy be hanged as traitors. The crowd whooped and hollered its approval.

A few days later, Lincoln called Johnson to join him in a tour of the Confederate capital. For a mile and half they walked through the ruins of Richmond. Then on April 9, Lee surrendered to Grant at Appomattox Court House, Virginia. A few more skirmishes would take place here and there. But for all practical purposes, the Civil War was over.

Just five days after Lee surrendered the Army of Northern Virginia, a group of conspirators carried out a last desperate plan that they hoped might save the Confederacy after all.

On April 14, 1865, Good Friday, Johnson went to the White House to talk with Lincoln. The president was making plans for bringing the Southern states back into the Union. Johnson urged Lincoln not to be lenient with the traitors.

Meanwhile, John Wilkes Booth was making his own plans for Lincoln and Johnson. He and several others were staying at a boardinghouse run by Mrs. Mary Surratt. There they had first planned to abduct the president. But soon their plans went even further. Booth was a confirmed Confederate. In a last-ditch effort to keep the Southern cause—and the war—alive, he plotted the murders of several top government officials. He would assassinate Lincoln. Lewis Paine was to murder Secretary of State Seward. A carriage-maker named George B. Atzerodt was assigned to kill Johnson.

That afternoon, Atzerodt took a room in the Kirkwood Hotel just above the room where Johnson was staying. He hid his weapons in his room, then went downstairs to the bar to have a drink.

President and Mrs. Lincoln were scheduled to attend the play *Our American Cousin* at Ford's Theatre that night. That afternoon, Lincoln confided to a friend, "It has been advertised that we will be there, and I cannot disappoint the people. Otherwise I would not go. I do not want to go."

That evening, ex-governor of Wisconsin Leonard Farwell, who was also staying at the Kirkwood, stopped by Johnson's room for a chat. He was on his way to Ford's Theatre, too, but Johnson declined to go. Instead, he got ready for bed.

Atzerodt, however, had lost his nerve. He wandered from saloon to saloon, getting drunker and drunker, then spent the rest of the night riding wildly about the Washington streets on horseback.

Unaware of the danger, Johnson read until he fell asleep.

At the same time, John Wilkes Booth was at Ford's Theatre. President Lincoln's guard had stepped away for a moment. The president's box was unguarded. Booth crept up to the door and looked through a tiny peephole he had secretly drilled through the wood that morning. When he saw the president, he silently stepped into the box. It was 10 o'clock when he fired a pistol at close range into the back of the president's head. Then Booth leapt down to the stage, breaking his leg in the fall. To the audience, he shouted "*Sic semper tyrannis!*" which is Latin for "Thus always with tyrants!" Then he stumbled through the wings of the stage to the alley behind the theater and made his escape on horseback.

The president's box at Ford's Theatre, in which Abraham Lincoln was shot to death.

The audience was in an uproar. Screams and shouts filled the theater and carried into the night as people ran into the streets. Lincoln, wounded but still alive, was carried across the street to the Petersen Boarding House, where doctors did everything possible to save his life.

Meanwhile, Governor Farwell ran the two and a half blocks through the hysterical crowds to the Kirkwood Hotel. He pounded on the door to Johnson's room. He climbed up and shouted through the transom, "Governor Johnson, if you are in the room, I must see you!"

At last the sleepy vice-president opened the door. "Someone has shot and murdered the President!" Farwell shouted. The two men clung to each other a moment for support. A few of Johnson's friends also came in. Guards were placed by the door as Johnson sent Farwell to find out about Lincoln's condition. When he returned, he reported that Lincoln was dying. Secretary Seward had been stabbed in his bed. No one knew what other madness might be stalking the streets of Washington.

At two A.M., despite protests, Johnson walked with Farwell and Major James O'Beirne to the Petersen Boarding House. In a back bedroom, Johnson found Lincoln lying unconscious on a bed that was much too small for him. The room was filled with doctors and members of the cabinet. Mrs. Lincoln's hysterical screams could be heard from the next room. Johnson stayed no more than a half-hour. Then he returned to his rooms at the Kirkwood.

Abraham Lincoln died at 7:22 the next morning. It was a gray, drizzly day. The city that had so recently celebrated joyously was now plunged into the darkest depression. At Johnson's request, Chief Justice Salmon P. Chase came to the Kirkwood to administer the oath of office. Johnson appeared grief-stricken but calm and self-possessed. At 10 o'clock, Andrew Johnson—vice-president for only 41 days—was sworn in as the 17th president of the United States.

Johnson spoke briefly, in low dignified tones. "Toil and an honest advocacy of the great principles of free government have been my lot. The duties have been mine—the consequences God's. This has been the foundation of my political creed. . . . I want your encouragement and countenance. I shall ask and rely on you and others in carrying the government through its present perils."

The cabinet members who now stood around him had been shocked by Johnson's behavior at the inauguration. Now they were impressed and reassured by Johnson's serious, dignified manner. The newspapers that had carried outraged tales of his earlier embarrassing behavior now praised him.

Andrew Johnson, the "Mechanic President," at the time he took office.

The Greeneville tailor was 56 years old. Before him lay the greatest challenge of his life—one of the greatest ever faced by an American president. A Southerner who had branded his Confederate neighbors traitors, he had to find a way to put the broken nation back together.

AFTERMATH

"Johnson, we have faith in you. By the Gods,
there will be no trouble now in running the
government."
OHIO SENATOR BEN WADE, MEETING WITH JOHNSON
THE DAY AFTER LINCOLN DIED

The war that many had thought would be a three-month brawl had finally ended after four years of unimaginable bloodshed. The United States of America—less than a hundred years old—had been shaken. The country as it once was had been painfully destroyed.

The North celebrated victory. The South, though mourning its lost cause, found some relief in the end of the death and destruction. Yet heartache and bitterness would run deep on both sides for generations.

More than 600,00 men had died—a greater death toll than all other American wars put together. A whole generation of brave, hopeful young men had been lost.

In the North and the South, thousands of families had lost fathers, sons, brothers, and husbands in the war. Many families had wept to read the names of their sons on the death lists. Some men simply never came home, and many were buried in unmarked graves in distant states. It was an era when women were not supposed to work outside the home, were not allowed to vote, and were usually protected and taken care of by their men in almost every way. Thousands of young widows mourned their dead husbands as they wondered how in the world they would feed and clothe their children. Thousands of unmarried women mourned the death of their sweethearts—and the home and family that would never be.

The Southern economy had been destroyed. The men who did struggle home from the war found their small farms and homes in ruins, or their families impoverished and starving. Many soldiers came home wounded, their health ruined, unable to work because of illness or lost arms or legs or eyes. But even those who returned eager to go to work and try to put their tattered lives back together found little hope. Vast acres of farmland had been neglected. Great cities such as Atlanta and Richmond lay in the ruins. The railroads were in a shambles, and the banks were closed. Many of the huge plantations that had grown cotton—the South's major cash crop—had been abandoned or burned to the ground.

But there was suddenly no one to work the endless fields anyway. Four million slaves, who had worked the great plantations, had been set free. Their right to freedom was undeniable. But most had been kept ignorant and had been treated, at best, as children. Most had been barred from learning to read or write. Few owned property of any kind. They had no land to farm. And even the most menial jobs were almost impossible to find, for many whites had no money to pay workers. Many black families had been broken apart as mothers, fathers, sons, and daughters had been sold off to distant plantations before the war. They had been granted their freedom from slavery, but they were still not completely free. For they were given little help in learning how to live in a world that still treated them as inferior human beings.

The whole country was wounded and weary. Somehow a new nation had to be built from the ruins. This was the work that Andrew Johnson faced as president.

Abraham Lincoln had had great compassion for the Southern people. He had not planned to punish them. He believed that they—and all American people—had suffered enough. For the good of the nation as a whole, he had planned to bring the Secessionist states quickly back into the Union. He had fought long

Shanties like this one were the only housing that most newly-liberated African American families could afford.

and hard in Congress with politicians who opposed his charitable plans.

Then Lincoln was assassinated. Many Northerners blamed the South. Their bitterness toward Southerners grew. Many demanded that the rebels be severely punished. Many looked to the new president with great hope. For Johnson, the Southerner who had stood by the Union, had long branded his Southern neighbors traitors. Now it was his duty to lead the country through a "reconstruction," to bring all the states back into the system of government outlined in the Constitution of the United States. There were also thousands of freed slaves whose freedom and welfare were in question. Northerners believed Johnson would use a sterner hand in punishing the rebellious Confederates.

The Radical Republicans in Congress wasted no time. On the morning of Easter Sunday, April 16, the Congressional Committee on the Conduct of the War met with Johnson in the White House. Lincoln had been dead less than 48 hours. He had not even been buried yet.

Many Republicans had totally disagreed with Lincoln's compassionate attitude toward the South. They believed the Southern states had completely left the Union and had created a new country. The Confederacy had waged war against the United States—had lost—and should be treated as a defeated nation. The Radicals now quickly sought to press their views upon the new president. Ben Wade, spokesman for the committee, told the president: "Johnson, we have faith in you. By the Gods, there will be no trouble now in running the government."

Johnson's bitterness over Lincoln's assassination had hardened his feelings toward the Confederates. He may also have been flattered by the committee's high opinion of him. "I am very much obliged to you gentlemen," said Johnson. "I can only say that you can judge of my policy by the past. Everybody knows what that is. I hold this."

Then Johnson spoke in the bold, angry speechmaking style he used whenever called on to speak of the Rebels: "I hold that robbery is a crime," he told the committee. "Rape is a crime; murder is a crime; treason is a crime; and crime must be punished. . . . Treason must be made infamous, and traitors must be impoverished."

The Radicals went away delighted. They were confident that at last they had a president who would handle the reconstruction of the nation *their* way. Johnson, however, had made no promises, nor, had he committed himself to any proposal. In those first days of his

This drawing depicts President Andrew Johnson's first cabinet meeting.

presidency, he would tell visitors his policy "would unfold page by page."

Johnson quickly settled down to his work as president. Mrs. Lincoln, still hysterical over the death of her husband, had asked through her son if she could stay in the White House until she had recovered. Johnson graciously agreed and went to stay at a friend's home. But perhaps he might have thought twice if he had known it would be two months before she would be gone.

For now the president set up his office in a room in the treasury department. Seven days a week, he rose at six to read papers, had breakfast at 7:30, then went to his office. His day was cluttered with the paperwork of the presidency: There were letters to be answered and political appointments to be made. There were army promotions and discharges to handle.

And all Americans seemed to believe it their duty to tell the new president by letter or in person how he should handle the Rebels. People flocked to his waiting room to ask for pardons, complain about confiscated property, or handle a variety of other war-related problems. One by one, he handled the most important requests. Lunch was tea and crackers at his desk. In the afternoon, the doors were thrown open to allow anyone and everyone else in. The *Washington Star*, in an article titled "A President's Busy Day," said the scene looked a lot like a crowd "at the post-office window.... The President's manner at such times was always pleasant and gave confidence to the most timid. His decisions were quick and every individual who laid his case before him learned in half a dozen courteous words the final decision..."

When everyone had been seen, Johnson went back to work until dinnertime, at four o'clock. Then he returned to his office and worked on until 11 at night. Johnson had no hobbies; he did not go to the theater, and he had no interest in the society parties that filled the Washington evenings with light. The presidency was his work and his pleasure.

Meanwhile, in May, the conspirators in Lincoln's assassination had been rounded up and brought to trial. John Wilkes Booth had been shot and killed on April 25, 11 days after Lincoln's assassination, when soldiers tried to capture him in Virginia. The nation was calling out for revenge. War secretary Stanton insisted he had proof that high-ranking officials in the Confederate army were involved. His "proof" was later rejected, but he convinced Johnson to issue a warrant for the arrest of President Jefferson Davis and other Confederate leaders. Johnson offered a reward of $100,000 for Davis's capture. He then asked General Grant's advice on whether General Robert E. Lee might be arrested, too. Many Northerners demanded it, but Grant said it would be shameful and talked the president out of it. Grant and others felt Lee and his generals had simply been doing what they believed to be their duty, and that the suffering they had undergone in fighting the war was punishment enough for what they had done.

The trial of the conspirators began on May 9th. The next day, Jefferson Davis was captured in Georgia. When he learned that Johnson accused him of conspiring to assassinate Lincoln, Davis replied: "Why, Johnson knows better than that. He knows I much prefer Lincoln as President, to him." Davis was put in chains and imprisoned without trial at Fort Monroe, Virginia, until 1867.

The conspirators' trial was emotional and speedy. A nation in mourning for its president wanted quick justice. It also wanted revenge. The military jury sentenced four to die: Lewis Paine, who had attacked Seward; David Herold; George Atzerodt, who had been assigned to murder Johnson; and Mrs. Mary E. Surratt, who ran the boardinghouse where the plot was supposedly hatched. Three others received life imprisonment; another got six years.

The trial was fraught with puzzling information. The afternoon of the assassination, a man who looked like Booth had gone to the Kirkwood House and asked if Andrew Johnson was in. The clerk replied that Johnson was out. The man scribbled a note on a card, and the clerk had left it in the box of Johnson's secretary. "Don't want to disturb you are you at home? [sic]" It was signed, "J. Wilkes Booth." Handwriting experts confirmed that the hand–writing was indeed that of the man who had assassinated President Lincoln. The note was never explained.

Many people sought a pardon for Mrs. Surratt. They claimed that Booth's original plan had been simply to kidnap Lincoln in an effort to give the South a final chance to rally. Only later did the plan change to include assassination. Mrs. Surratt's supporters claimed she had no knowledge of the plot.

A request for pardon was supposedly sent to Johnson. But at the time, he was ill with bilious fever. He was gotten out of bed to sign the death warrant. But he claimed later that he never saw a request for pardon.

On July 7, under a blistering sun, Herold, Paine, Atzerodt, and

Mrs. Surratt were taken to the gallows and hanged as thousands looked on.

The curtain had fallen on the public drama of the trial of Lincoln's assassins. The public and the press were pleased with the ending.

During all these weeks, however, Johnson had been busy with other postwar issues. He was formulating the policies that would drive his administration. And he was coming to some conclusions that were soon to shock the nation.

Twelve days after Confederate president Jefferson Davis was captured, Johnson called off the blockades of most Southern ports.

On May 23 and 24, Union troops who had fought under Grant and Sherman paraded past the White House before a cheering crowd. A poised Johnson stood on a platform with other government officials and presided over the celebration. His popularity had never been stronger.

Five days later, President Johnson took a stand that would ultimately lead to his political disgrace.

RECONSTRUCTION

> "I love the Southern people. I know them to be brave and honorable, I know that they have accepted the situation and will come back into the Union in good faith."
>
> ANDREW JOHNSON

n May 26, 1865, the Southern Unionist Andrew Johnson shocked many Northerners by announcing a blanket policy of amnesty and pardon for the South.

"To the end . . . that the authority of the government of the United States may be restored and that peace, order and freedom be established, I, Andrew Johnson, President of the United States, do . . . hereby grant to all persons who have . . . participated in the existing rebellion, amnesty and pardon with restoration of all rights of property except as to slaves. . . . " Confederates would be granted U.S. citizenship if they took an oath of loyalty to the United States and swore to support and defend the Constitution.

There were, of course, some exceptions. Fourteen classes of rebels—such as high-level military officers in the Confederate army, governors of the seceded states, and all officers educated at West Point or Annapolis—were required to apply individually for amnesty. Johnson added only one class that Lincoln had not already proposed: All persons who had been a part of the rebellion and whose taxable property was more than $20,000, a sizable sum in the 1860s.

IMPORTANT EVENTS OF RECONSTRUCTION, 1865–1877

Year	Events
1865	President Johnson begins reconstruction of the Union, suddenly changing his position against former rebels and, to the dismay of many Northerners, begins freely pardoning Confederate leaders.
	The Freedman's Bureau is established to assist former slaves.
	Southern states enact Black Codes aimed at controlling the newly freed black people.
	The Thirteenth Amendment is ratified.
1866	The Civil Rights Act is passed, over Johnson's veto, denying the states the power to restrict former slaves' rights to testify in court and to hold property.
	Most Southern states reject the proposed Fourteenth Amendment, which grants black persons U.S. citizenship.
1868	The House of Representatives impeaches Johnson. He is found not guilty by the Senate.
	Seven out of eleven Southern states have been readmitted to the Union by this year.
	The Fourteenth Amendment is ratified.
	Ulysses S. Grant is elected president.
1870	Congress passes three Force Acts, placing elections under federal jurisdiction in response to Southern whites' intimidation of black and white Republican voters. Violence and other threats continue.
	The Fifteenth Amendment is ratified, granting blacks the right to vote, although eight Northern states have rejected bills granting blacks this right.
	The four remaining Confederate states are readmitted to the Union.
1872	The Amnesty Act is passed, pardoning most remaining former rebels.
	Grant is re-elected.
1874	The Democrats win a majority in the House of Representatives.
1875	Several Grant appointees are charged with corruption, undermining his administration.
	The second Civil Rights Act bars segregation in public facilities but lacks enforcement. It is declared unconstitutional in 1883.
1876	By this time, a total of 632 black legislators have taken office in former Confederate states. South Carolina has the most black legislators, with 190. Only Tennessee has failed to elect a single black legislator.
	The presidential election, between Samuel B. Tilden (Democrat) and Rutherford B. Hayes (Republican), is disputed.
1877	Southern Democrats in the House of Representatives offer to vote for Rutherford B. Hayes, in exchange for the withdrawal of federal troops from the South. Hayes agrees and is elected. The Democratic party becomes all-powerful in the South, with blacks' newfound rights being abandoned.

Southern critics charged that with this rule, Johnson was unfairly taking vengeance on the rich slave-owning aristocrats. An 1865 Virginia delegation urged its repeal. According to Johnson's biographer Robert W. Winston, Johnson asked one delegate if he was unaware "that men aided the rebellion according to the extent of their pecuniary [financial] means."

"No, I do not know it," the delegate answered.

"Why, yes, you do," said the president, who had been born in poverty. "You know perfectly well it was the wealthy men of the South who dragooned [forced] the people into Secession."

In the six weeks that he had served as president, Johnson had spoken with hundreds of individuals from all over the country. He had listened to politicians from the North and from the South, to soldiers who had worn blue and soldiers who had worn gray, to mothers seeking amnesty for sons, to lawyers, pastors, and farmers. He had studied Lincoln's plans and the proposals of those who had opposed him. And he had examined his own long-held belief in the Union, the Constitution, and the honesty of the common working man.

Johnson would never forgive the leaders of the Confederacy. But in the end, he chose a path of compassion and forgiveness for the people of the South. He believed leniency would most quickly and thoroughly put the war to rest so Americans could go on with the work of rebuilding the nation. Over the next nine months, he personally interviewed and pardoned 14,000 leading Southerners.

Johnson also issued a plan for bringing former Confederate states back into the Union. One by one, the states had seceded. One by one, each state would have to restore its government and be readmitted to the Union. On the same day that he issued his proclamation of amnesty, Johnson issued a plan for restoring the Union. It applied specifically to the state where he was born, North Carolina, but it was the model that would apply to other states. It appointed William W. Holden provisional governor to oversee the recreation of a new state government. The former Southern governors were now unable to serve because they had been rebels—traitors in the eyes of the U.S. Once the people elected their own leaders, the provisional governors would have to step down.

Over the next two months, Johnson issued similar proclamations for six other Southern states. The president believed the remaining rebellious states, including Tennessee, had already demonstrated that they were making progress on their own. In doing this, Johnson acted on his own, since Congress was not yet in session. The Radical Republicans were shocked. The Conservatives were relieved. He made friends and enemies among the people in both the North and South. Robert E. Lee called Johnson "first in the field with a Reconstruction policy. . . . Everyone approves of Johnson's policy." By contrast, Radical Republican Thaddeus Stevens joked that "If something is not done, the President will be crowned king before Congress meets." Stevens believed the Southern states should be treated as a conquered nation.

Johnson and his family had at last moved into the White House. It was a comfort to have his wife Eliza with him; his rise in politics and the war had so often kept them apart. But Eliza had suffered for many years from what doctors diagnosed as "pthisis" or "consumption," a slow, progressive form of tuberculosis. Now she was more or less an invalid and would spend most of her White House years reading or knitting in the family's quarters on the second floor. She still loved to look after and spoil her husband, but she was unable to perform the official role of first lady.

The Johnsons were lucky to have a wonderful substitute in their daughter Martha Johnson Patterson. Her husband, David T. Patterson, had recently been elected a U.S. senator from Tennessee. So the Pattersons moved into the White House with their children Mary Belle and Andrew. The Johnsons' widowed daughter Mary Johnson Stover moved in, too, and brought her children Lillie, Sarah, and Andrew. Along with Andrew Johnson's 12-year-old son Andrew, Jr., the house was filled with children—and filled with Andrews! Often they would burst in on "Grandpa" while he was working in his office. And only they could sometimes pull him away from this White House duties for an afternoon picnic in the country.

In the role of first lady, Mrs. Patterson brought an air of grace, dignity, and common sense to the White House, which was in a shambles after the war. Mrs. Patterson worked hard to make it a comfortable, presentable home. She dressed in calico and kept the rooms of the White House filled with fresh-cut flowers. She bought two jersey cows to graze on the lawn and provide the family with fresh milk. "We are plain people from the mountains of Tennessee," she declared, "called here for a short time by a national calamity. I trust too much will not be expected of us."

Johnson's 31-year-old son Robert came to Washington, too, but he brought his father only trouble. He went to work for his father as a private secretary. But Robert had a severe drinking problem that brought the president worry and embarrassment.

As Johnson worked to steer the troubled nation back on course, his popularity grew in North and South. The *New York Herald* wrote: "We can assure him that he is universally regarded...as the proper man for the crisis," and later: "We are content with the reconstruction policy proclaimed by President Johnson. It is a practical program...it will be supported by the country." Even foreign nations praised him as a man of peace. On October 13, 1865, Johnson declared, "We are making very rapid progress—so rapid I sometimes cannot realize it. It appears like a dream!"

Johnson's optimism would soon be crushed, however, as the Radical Republicans watched the unfolding of his policies with surprise and dismay. It seemed to them that Johnson was not going to be as strict with the South as they had hoped.

Meanwhile, Johnson encouraged the Southern states to ratify the 13th Amendment.

> Neither slavery nor involuntary servitude...shall exist within the United States, or any place subject to their jurisdiction.

Most states eventually followed Johnson's lead and adopted the amendment. By December, two-thirds of the states had ratified the amendment, and became part of the Constitution. The institution of slavery in the United States was at last coming to an end. Some four million slaves were now free.

Americans had a golden opportunity before them. They could at last make the words of the Declaration of Independence come true in fact as well as in theory:

> We hold these truths to be self-evident, that all men are created equal, that they are endowed by their Creator with certain inalienable rights, that among these are life, liberty, and the pursuit of happiness.

But Andrew Johnson let this golden opportunity slip through the nation's fingers.

Johnson had always spoken out against the white aristocrats who owned slaves. He believed they created a society that suppressed the poor white working man as well as the black slave. In 1864, while running for vice-president, he had declared before a rally of whites and blacks: "I will indeed be your Moses, and lead you through the Red Sea of war and bondage to a fairer state of liberty and peace."

In spite of this, Johnson, like a majority of people North and South in the 1860s, still believed that whites were superior to blacks. Johnson was against slavery. But he differed with the Radicals one key issue: He did not believe that free black men should be given the right to vote. The issue should not get in the way of the more important issue of reconstructing the nation. Many Northern Radicals were outraged: How could blacks be considered free and still be denied the right to vote? Of course, the issue applied only to men, for even white women were denied the right to vote until 1920.

Johnson, however, stubbornly clung to his belief that voting rights were a state issue. He believed that the federal government had no right to interfere with individual states' rights. Most of all, Johnson did not want this issue to stand in the way of quickly reuniting the Union. Even in the North, only five states allowed blacks to vote on the same basis as whites. Blacks were only a small percentage of the population, and yet in states such as Minnesota, Wisconsin, and Connecticut, new laws giving blacks the vote were soundly defeated.

Meanwhile, Johnson's lenient policies toward the Confederate states began to backfire. In the spring of 1865, at the end of the war, Americans expected that Johnson would be harsh with the Confederate "traitors." The defeated Southerners were on their knees, willing to agree to almost any terms in order to be allowed to rejoin the Union.

Then, over the summer, Johnson's plans became clear. His plans were actually similar to those Lincoln had proposed. Johnson would be generous and forgiving with the Southern people. There would be no severe punishments. The South sighed with relief.

And now, with little to fear, some Southern leaders began to carve out their own path on the road to Reconstruction. Johnson urged the states to elect representatives in the fall elections, who could take the "Ironclad Oath": swearing that they had never voluntarily aided the Confederacy and that they were loyal to the Union. While the upper Southern states seemed to follow his advice, states in the Deep South actually elected several ex-Confederate generals and colonels to office.

Many of the Southern state legislators now moved to enact "Black Codes"—harsh laws defining the freed slaves' place in society. The codes did give freed slaves rights to own property, marry, make contracts, and testify in court against other blacks. (Blacks were still not allowed to testify against whites.) But the codes also sought to restrict freed slaves to farm work and create fines and punishments for everything from vagrancy, to "insulting" gestures or language, to "malicious mischief." In Mississippi each January, all blacks had to show written proof that they had work for the coming year. If they broke contracts, they could be arrested by whites. Apprentice laws could force young black orphans to work for their former white owners without pay. Other laws kept blacks from owning guns, restricted fishing rights, and made stealing a horse a capital crime. Freed slaves paid taxes, but usually could not use the schools, parks, and services for the poor that were paid for by those tax dollars. These laws were enforced by white officials. Accused criminals were tried by white juries. Often whites were not prosecuted for crimes against blacks.

Black codes had a short life; most of these laws would be repealed by the end of 1866. Many Southerners agreed that they were an attempt to re-establish "slavery in all but its name," as Virginia's General Alfred H. Terry put it.

But the black codes had a powerful effect on the attitudes of both North and South. It was a critical time in the healing of the war's wounds; these negative laws worked only to divide the country.

Northerners were shocked by the black codes. They believed they allowed whites to treat blacks almost as badly as if they were still slaves.

"As for Negro suffrage," said Chicago editor Charles A. Dana, "the mass of the Union men in the Northwest do not care a great deal. What scares them is the idea that the rebels are all to be let back . . . and made a power in the government again, just as though there had been no rebellion."

Johnson did not deny that there were problems. But he continued to insist, "We can't undertake to run state governments in all these Southern states. Their people must do that, though I reckon at first they may do it badly."

However, after the elections, even Johnson saw that things were not working out exactly as he had planned. "There seems, in many of the elections, something like defiance, which is all out of place at this time." Southerners voted many ex-Confederates into office—including Confederate vice-president Alexander H. Stephens.

Reconstruction was not going as anyone—especially President Johnson—had though it would. The nation seemed to find itself at a crossroads with no signposts.

13

A NATION REBUILT

"I know very well that this policy
is attended with some risk.... But
it is a risk that must be taken."
PRESIDENT JOHNSON, DECEMBER 1865

inally, Andrew Johnson made a bid to end the stalemate. When Congress met in December 1865, the president made an eloquent speech to thank God for "the preservation of the United States." Of the states in the Union he said, "The whole cannot exist without the parts, nor the parts without the whole. So long as the Constitution of the United States endures, the States will endure. The destruction of one is the destruction of the other; the preservation of one is the preservation of the other.... It has been my steadfast object...to derive a healing policy from the fundamental and unchanging principles of the Constitution. Johnson continued, "I found the States suffering from the effects of the civil war. Resistance to the General Government appeared to have exhausted itself."

Then he went on to explain his policies since taking office. "All pretended acts of secession were from the beginning null and void." Johnson believed that the states had no constitutional right to secede; thus they had never actually left the Union. Their governments had, instead, been unlawfully taken over by hostile rebels, "their functions suspended, but not destroyed." Johnson argued that his restoration policies were intended to help the citizens of these states resume their constitutional rights. "I know very well that this policy is attended with some risk.... But it is a risk that must be taken."

Johnson defended his decision to allow each state to decide the issue of the black vote. But he also said that the nation must "avoid hasty assumptions of any natural impossibility for the two races to live side by side in a state of mutual benefit and good will.... Let us then, go on and make the experiment in good faith, and not be too easily disheartened. The country is in need of labor, and the freedmen are in need of employment, culture, and protection.... Let there be nothing wanting to the fair trial of the experiment."

The president's remarks were praised by the press at home and abroad. The *New York Times* called Johnson's words "full of wisdom." The *Nation* said that Americans could be proud of such a document written by "this Tennessee tailor who was toiling for his daily bread in the humblest of employments when the chiefs of all other countries were reaping every advantage which school, college or social position could furnish."

But Thaddeus Stevens had warned Johnson a few days before that he must change his stand—or lose the support of the Northern Republics. The President made his choice, and in doing so, made enemies who would seek his downfall.

On December 4, the 39th Congress met for the first time. In the House of Representatives, clerk Edward McPherson called the roll—and left out the names of representatives from the rebel states, including Tennessee. The Northern states were determined not to admit the Southerners.

"If Tennessee is not in the Union, and is not a loyal state," demanded New York Congressman James Brooks, "and if the people of Tennessee are aliens and foreigners in the Union, by what right does the President of the United States usurp a place in the White House?"

But the Radicals refused to listen to the objections—on the basis that the Southerners were not proper members of Congress. "The attitude of Congress is as plain as the sun's pathway in the heavens," Johnson exclaimed. "The door having been shut in the rebels' faces, it is still to be kept bolted." The Radicals then created a Joint Committee on Reconstruction to oversee "all measures dealing with the South."

Early in 1866, Congress passed two bills that would further its battle with the president. The first bill proposed extending the role of the Freedman's Bureau, and the second concerned civil rights for blacks. The Freedman's Bureau had been created in March 1865 to help ease blacks' transition from slavery to a life of freedom. It was designed to distribute food, clothing, and fuel to needy freedmen, set up schools, and oversee the conditions of blacks in the South. It took abandoned and confiscated farmland in the South and divided it into small farms for the freedmen. One of its greatest achievements was the creation of thousands of schools and the hiring of thousands of teachers to teach ex-slaves how to read and write. It was not unusual to see three generations of blacks studying their primers together in an abandoned building that had once been used as a slave auction house. Freedman's Bureau funds helped found some of the nation's first black universities.

Some Northern Congressmen thought the Freedman's Bureau should be a permanent cabinet-level agency. Others believed it had a transitional role.

Johnson surprised everyone and vetoed the Freedman's Bureau Bill. He agreed that the bureau had served a proper purpose during the last months of the war. But he did not believe in expanding its powers. The government did not hand out public money, set up schools, or buy land for the millions of poor hard working whites. Doing so for freed slaves, Johnson believed, would teach them that they did not have to work for a living. Besides, how could he sign a law affecting the South when the Southern states had not been allowed to vote on it?

The Radicals in Congress were outraged. The next day, Congress responded by passing a resolution that would continue to keep the rebel states out. As Thaddeus Stevens put it, "Rebel

Congressmen would be admitted when Congress said so, not before."

On Washington's birthday, Johnson went against his advisers and spoke out at a rally of well-wishers: "When I perceive... men—I care not by what name you call them—still opposed to the Union, I am free to say to you I am still with the people. I am still for the preservation of these States, for the preservation of this Union, and in favor of this great Government accomplishing its destiny."

Voices in the crowd called out for him to name names, to identify those people he thought were against the Union. "Suppose I should name to you those I look upon as being opposed to the fundamental principles of this Government, and as now laboring to destroy them. I say Thaddeus Stevens, of Pennsylvania; I say Charles Sumner of Massachusetts; I say Wendell Phillips of Massachusetts."

In March 1866, Congress sent Johnson the Civil Rights Bill. It declared that all people born in the United States (except Native Americans) were citizens of the United States. And it said that the freed slaves must have "the same rights of property and person" as whites.

Johnson stubbornly vetoed this bill too. How could such a major issue be passed into law when 11 of the 36 states were still barred from Congress? Also, the matters dealt with in the bill were legal questions that had always been left up to the states. In addition, Johnson said that special treatment of blacks by the federal government in effect discriminated against whites.

With this veto, Johnson lost much of his support in Congress. And it turned the rift between him and the Radical Republicans into a full-scale war. Over the next few months, the Republicans would push through other legislation, attempting to overthrow Johnson's policy and place the South under military rule. Johnson vetoed many of these bills. "The wicked rebel has been put down by the strong army of the Government, but now another rebellion has started," he declared, "a rebellion to overthrow the Constitution and revolutionize the Government."

In April, the Senate and the House of Representatives passed the Civil Rights Bill over Johnson's veto. It was the first major law ever passed over a presidential veto.

In June, Congress passed the 14th Amendment, one of the most important amendments to the Constitution. Its aim was to guarantee that all U.S. citizens would be equal before the law—and that no individual state could pass laws that would interfere with that right. Its second clause was a direct attack on Southern policies on voting rights. States that denied voting rights to black males would have their representation in Congress reduced. The third clause prevented rebels from holding office. And the fourth prevented the United States or any individual state government from paying off any debt acquired during the rebellion against the Union, including the loss of money from the freeing of slaves.

Some critics said this admitted that an individual state had the right to deny blacks the right to vote. Feminists objected to putting the word *males* into the Constitution. They believed that it was time to give all Americans—black, white, male, and female—the right to vote. Those who praised the amendment saw it as a new stage in American government: where no state could pass laws that would undermine the Bill of Rights and the Constitution.

Johnson was violently opposed to the amendment. Congress had passed it as a direct attack on his policies, he believed. And he said that the people should have been consulted. Congress was beginning to ignore his opinions. The *New York Tribune* wrote: "Mr. Johnson rode his hobby [toy horse] into Congress yesterday. Nobody wanted him, nobody expected him, nobody felt he had any business there. His message was about as appropriate as though it had contained the bill of fare for his breakfast, his latest tailor's account, or his opinions upon the cause of thunder."

In July, Congress passed a new Freedman's Bureau Act. Johnson once again vetoed it. This time, however, Congress quickly overrode his veto and turned it into law.

Meanwhile, Johnson's hope for a peaceful reunification of the nation was fading. In May, in Memphis, Tennessee, two horse-drawn carriages ran into each other on a busy street. One driver was white; the other was black. Crowds gathered as the white policeman arrested the black driver. Some black veterans protested the action, and violence broke out. For the next three days, white mobs roamed the streets assaulting blacks. Gangs of whites attacked the shanties in South Memphis, where black soldiers and their families lived. By the time the violence ended, at least 47 black men lay dead, and more than 80 were wounded. Five black women had been raped. Homes and churches had been looted and burned to the ground.

In late July, race riots broke out in New Orleans. Ex-Confederates were becoming a major power in the state. Now Governor James M. Wells backed a Radical plan to reconvene the state constitutional convention to create a new state government and give blacks the right to vote. Twenty-five delegates arrived for the convention. Nearly 200 black supporters turned out to show their support. Conservatives showed up to prevent the meeting. Fights broke out, and soon shots were fired. Federal troops were called in to stop the rioting. Before it was all over, 34 blacks and 3 white Radicals were dead, and at least 100 people had been injured. Johnson blamed the Radicals. But Northerners pointed to the violence as proof that Johnson's Reconstruction policies had failed.

By August, Johnson decided to carry his side of this political struggle to the people. He went off on what was called his "Swing 'Round the Circle." Secretary of State Seward, General Ulysses S. Grant, and other national leaders went with him. Baltimore, Philadelphia, New York, Niagara Falls, St. Louis, Indianapolis— for 2,000 miles the president traveled by train, campaigning for candidates who would back, not battle, his policies. "I fought those in the South who commenced the rebellion, and now I opposed those in the North who are trying to break up the Union. I am for the Union, the whole Union, and nothing but the Union."

At first his speeches were cheered. Then the Radicals began planting people in the crowds to jeer the president and call him a traitor, or to try to prevent him from speaking. Republican newspapers misreported his speeches and ran political cartoons that made fun of him. Johnson faced the hecklers and the criticism with determination and the conviction that he was in the right. "I have been fighting the South and they have been whipped and crushed, and they acknowledge their defeat and accept the terms of the Constitution; and now as I go around the circle, having fought traitors in the South, I am prepared to fight traitors in the North."

But Johnson often let himself be drawn into verbal sparring, which was a mistake. Many observers thought his off-the-cuff remarks were often embarrassing. Even his friends and supporters tried to get him to stop. But Johnson insisted on continuing his trip. In Indianapolis, the crowds shouted "Shut up!" and would not let him speak. In other towns, he was snubbed by local officials who refused to come out and greet him. Even worse, his endless speeches caused him to lose his most valuable asset: his strong speaking voice. He often grew hoarse trying to shout above the jeering crowds.

In the long run, his critics and supporters had to agree: He would have been better off if he had just stayed home.

It seemed Johnson's opponents were succeeding. The tide of public opinion was beginning to turn. In the November 1866 elections, the Republicans gained two-thirds control of Congress.

And the Radicals set out to bring the president down.

FIRST TASTE OF FREEDOM

"The right of citizens of the United States to vote shall not be denied or abridged by the United States or by any state on account of race, color, or previous condition of servitude."

15TH AMENDMENT TO THE CONSTITUTION

Andrew Johnson faced his enemies in Congress with dignity and stubbornness. He went head to head with them on the issues of Reconstruction, and always refused to compromise. While in office he vetoed 29 bills; Congress, now controlled by Radical Republicans, would override 15 by a two-thirds vote.

In February 1867, Thaddeus Stevens presented the first of four Reconstruction bills that would undo the work of Lincoln and Johnson. Known as the Reconstruction Act, this legislation divided the 10 Southern states into 5 military districts to be ruled by U.S. generals. To rejoin the Union, a state had to call a new constitutional convention made up of black and white delegates to rewrite the state's laws. It also had to guarantee blacks the right to vote, and ratify the 14th Amendment—which prevents any state from making any law that would abridge the rights of an individual as a citizen of the United States. Leaders of the Confederacy were barred from voting or holding public office. Federal troops were sent into the states to make sure that they complied with the law.

Southern mythology long held that it was a time of terror in the South, that Union soldiers stalked the streets. The myth said that

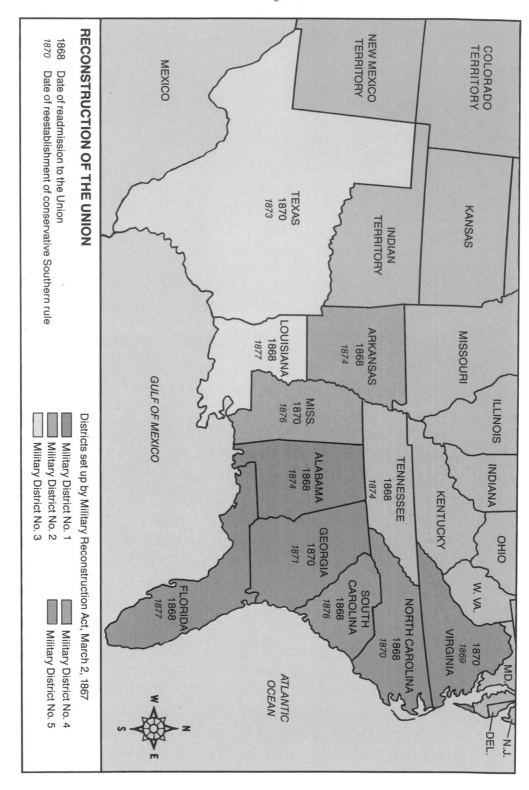

RECONSTRUCTION OF THE UNION

1868 Date of readmission to the Union
1870 Date of reestablishment of conservative Southern rule

Districts set up by Military Reconstruction Act, March 2, 1867

Military District No. 1
Military District No. 2
Military District No. 3
Military District No. 4
Military District No. 5

MEXICO

COLORADO TERRITORY

NEW MEXICO TERRITORY

KANSAS

INDIAN TERRITORY

TEXAS
1870
1873

MISSOURI

ILLINOIS

INDIANA

OHIO

ARKANSAS
1868
1874

LOUISIANA
1868
1877

GULF OF MEXICO

MISS.
1870
1876

ALABAMA
1868
1874

TENNESSEE
1868
1874

KENTUCKY

W. VA.

GEORGIA
1870
1871

FLORIDA
1868
1877

SOUTH CAROLINA
1868
1876

NORTH CAROLINA
1868
1870

VIRGINIA
1870
1869

MD.

N.J.

DEL.

ATLANTIC OCEAN

greedy low-class "carpetbaggers"—so-called because they carried all their belongings in a satchel made of carpet—swarmed into the South to take over the governments and to get rich off the defeated Southerners. It said that "scalawags"—Southern traitors who supported the Republicans—collaborated with the Yankees in ravishing the South, and that uneducated freedmen filled the state governments and played havoc with the law.

Southerners may well have felt "overrun" by unscrupulous carpetbaggers, scalawags, and freedmen. But this image is greatly exaggerated.

Many Northerners did come south to participate in Reconstruction, but, in fact, most were well-educated members of the middle class: lawyers, teachers, businessmen, Union soldiers, or employees of the Freedman's Bureau. Missionaries from Northern churches came out of a sense of duty to help the newly freed slaves. Educated freedmen came hoping to teach their Southern brothers and sisters and spread a new political message.

Surely some came to exploit the South, seeking profit or political opportunities. But many more came out of a true commitment to help the cause of the Southern blacks. They taught the freedmen to read and write and gave them lessons in history and government—preparing them to vote.

Southern blacks were not passive observers of this period of dramatic change. The Reconstruction Act inspired among these new citizens a passion for politics. Blacks flocked to hear both black and white lecturers from the North speak on civil rights, educational and economic reform, and the Republican philosophy. Black voters joined Union Leagues and other political organizations in droves. These groups were active in politics, but also raised money for the sick, built schools and churches, and went on strike for higher wages. Every picnic, church service, and meeting became an opportunity to discuss politics and civil rights. In Alabama, Florida, Mississippi, Louisiana, and South Carolina, the results were startling: More blacks than whites registered to vote in these states.

RECONSTRUCTION AND AFRICAN AMERICANS

The years following the Civil War were a time of great hope for African Americans. Slavery was abolished, and blacks in the South were promised equal status by northern congressmen known as Radical Republicans. Between 1868 and 1870, ten Southern states were readmitted to the Union. The states' governments were set up by "carpetbaggers." Named after the suitcases, or carpetbags, they carried, the carpetbaggers were northern politicians who went south to take advantage of the states' weakened condition. For the first time, blacks could vote, and they elected many black congressmen and senators. Many Southerners resented the new rights given to blacks, which included the right to sit on a jury and the right to an equal education. Secret hate societies formed, such as the Ku Klux Klan. In time, the angry Southerners gained power. The period of Reconstruction was nothing more than a brief vision of equality for blacks.

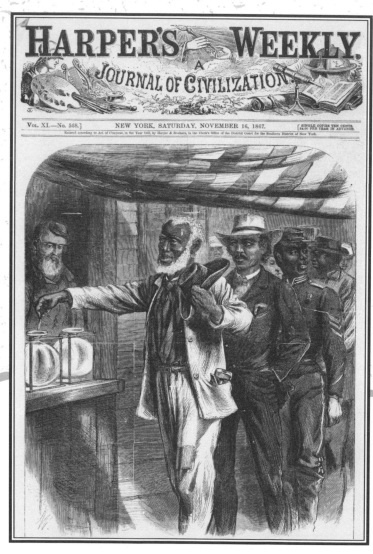

A hopeful sign: the cover of *Harper's Weekly* shows African Americans casting their first vote.

This political cartoon shows the Radical Republican view, mocking President Johnson's approach to Reconstruction.

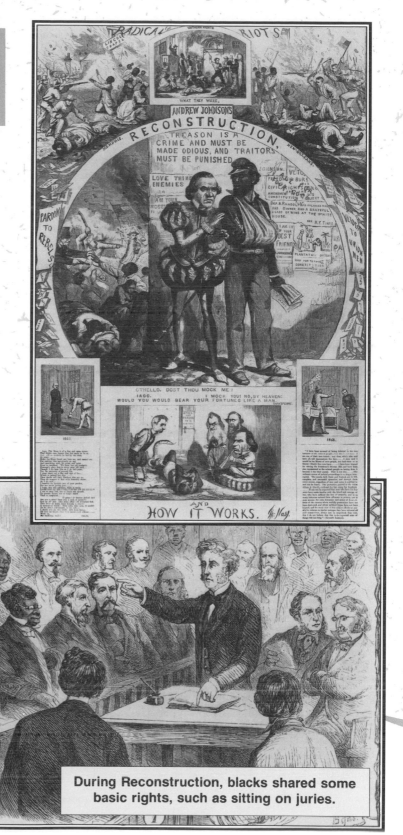

During Reconstruction, blacks shared some basic rights, such as sitting on juries.

In these small, enthusiastic groups were planted the seeds of a revolution. Blacks no longer had to stand by powerless and watch while white politicians debated the role of blacks in a white society. Now black slaves were free and had their own political voice. It would be a long, difficult road. A hundred years in the future, their descendants would still be fighting for political justice. But the struggle for black civil rights had begun.

Throughout the South, coalitions of black and white delegates began the work of rewriting the states' constitutions. In only one state—South Carolina—did black delegates outnumber whites. It was a new age with no rules. For decades, blacks and whites had dealt with each other in a master-slave relationship. Now they had to sit side by side and decide on laws that would be fair for all. Most blacks of that time did not demand social equality, but only argued for political and economic equal rights. Many whites learned to see blacks in a new light and work alongside them for a new order. But often those whites who did were jeered and called "scalawags" by some of their white neighbors.

Many of these new coalitions of blacks and whites made great improvements in how the laws treated both blacks and poorer whites. They passed fairer tax laws. Fewer crimes were now punishable by the death penalty. Laws that granted special rights to the large property owners of the South were repealed. Major changes were made in education. Schools had long excluded blacks and poor whites, liked the young Andrew Johnson, who could not pay to attend. Many of the new constitutions established public education open to all blacks and whites.

Meanwhile, many white Southerners feared the destruction of their society by "outsiders." They saw this Republican-dominated Reconstruction as a threat to their governments and their way of life. One outgrowth of this frustration was the emergence of secret societies such as the Knights of the White Camellia, the White Brotherhood, and the best-known, the Ku Klux Klan.

The Klan had been started in the spring of 1866 in Pulaski, Tennessee, by six former Confederate soldiers. At first it was a social club that provided aid to widows and orphans of Confederate soldiers. But soon its gatherings turned violent as Klan members began to take it upon themselves to terrorize the newly freed blacks and their Republican supporters. Other Klan "dens" sprang up across Tennessee and then spread across the South. By 1867, the Klan had grown into a violent anti-Reconstruction society. Its major goal was to restore the order of the Old South—and to re-establish white supremacy.

Klan members dressed in long, white robes and hid their faces beneath hoods. They developed rituals and held secret meetings. Members included ordinary farmers and laborers, merchants, lawyers, and even ministers. At first, fear was their weapon. But when they could not frighten their victims into doing what they wanted, they used violence to achieve their ends.

In the beginning, the Klan had been supported by the conservative press and many educated Southerners. But this changed as gradually the Klan developed into a vigilante terrorist group that used violence to support its ideas. Klan members went on midnight raids carrying flaming torches, and burned down the homes of blacks or their white supporters. They dragged blacks from their homes and whipped them for "crimes" such as insolence or voting. They attacked men, women, and children alike. Often the Klan specifically went after blacks who were doing well—successful farmers and businessmen—because they were changing the former role of blacks as powerless members of society. It also attacked blacks' white supporters, and anyone else whose improved economic status seemed to threaten their way of life. The Klan hoped to end Republican rule in the South.

During Reconstruction, many freedmen and white Republicans were murdered. But even for such extreme crimes, it was often difficult to prosecute Klan members. They swore an oath of secrecy; they attacked in the dark of night. And often they had friends within the law enforcement agencies and among the towns' most prominent citizens.

According the Colonel George W. Kirk of the U.S. Army, stationed in North Carolina:

> The juries were made up of Ku-Klu [sic], and it was impossible for any of the loyal people to get justice before the courts. Not less than

fifty or sixty persons have been killed by the Ku-Klux in the State, besides some three or four hundred whippings, and there has never been a man convicted that I have heard of.... Colored men cannot get justice.

By 1870, many Northerners and Southerners alike were outraged by the Klan's methods and called for its end. Even Imperial Wizard Nathan Bedford Forrest, the head of the KKK, claimed that it had gone far beyond its original mission and called for its disbandment. Congress passed tough new laws to suppress this reign of terror by the Ku Klux Klan and similar groups. But outbreaks of violence would continue.

The Klu Klux Klan used terrorist tactics to keep blacks from improving their social and economic status.

Whites who objected to equal rights for blacks also used other weapons in their fight against Republican Reconstruction. Sometimes white shopkeepers would refuse to sell goods to blacks or to whites known to be Republicans. It did not matter if an individual kept his voting preferences secret—because many newspapers published complete lists of those who voted Republican.

Often the only work available to a poor, uneducated ex-slave was sharecropping. Sharecroppers worked a white man's land with tools rented from the owner. When the crops came in, they owed as much as one-half or more of the crop in rent. And if a sharecropper could not read, it was difficult for him to know for sure if the landowner was keeping honest books. If the crops did poorly, the sharecroppers sank quickly into debt. Sometimes the white land-owners would hire only those workers who signed a contract promising that they would not join the Republican Party.

In 1870, the 15th Amendment became a part of the Constitution. One of the briefest amendments to the Constitution, it was one of the most important in American history:

> The right of citizens of the United States to vote shall not be denied or abridged by the United States or by any State on account of race, color, or previous condition of servitude.

Over the next 20 years—despite opposition that was often violent—22 black Southerners would be elected to Congress. Many were ex-slaves. Half had gone to college, in an age when many white lawmakers had not. In a time when blacks had been given few opportunities while they were starting out, these men held their own. James G. Blaine of Maine, who served first as a representative, then as Speaker of the House, and then as a senator during these years, said: "The colored men who took their seats in both the Senate and House did not appear ignorant or helpless. They were as a rule studious, earnest, ambitious men whose public conduct...would be honorable to any race."

Blacks in Congress would still endure discrimination nearly everywhere they went. They would often face ridicule and violence

The Fifteenth Amendment, celebrated in this poster, consisted of a single sentence giving blacks the vote.

just by taking office. But they would become an undeniable voice in Congress as they worked for civil rights, federal funding of education, and the rights of other oppressed people, such as Native Americans and Asian immigrants.

Unfortunately, the continuing violence across the South began to wear away at the progress made by blacks. By the 1870s, even Northerners would begin to support the idea of "home rule"—which really meant "white rule"—in the South. Federal troops were removed, and the North left the South to run its own government. Blacks lost all hope for a new order in the South. In 1879, an estimated 40,000 blacks migrated to Kansas. Many others traveled to New York City and then emigrated to Africa. Southern Democrats tried to block the black labor force from leaving in this "Exodus of 1879."

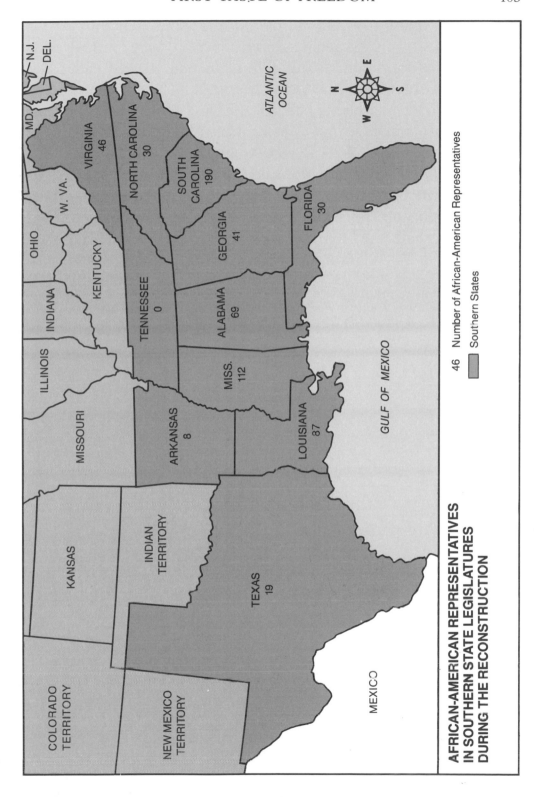

AFRICAN-AMERICAN REPRESENTATIVES IN SOUTHERN STATE LEGISLATURES DURING THE RECONSTRUCTION

46 Number of African-American Representatives

Southern States

With the return of white rule in the South, many of the achievements of blacks during Reconstruction were pushed aside and forgotten for a while. But a fundamental change had taken place: Black Americans had tasted freedom.

For the first time, blacks had stood in line with whites and cast their votes as citizens of the United States. They had proved their abilities as members of the government. They had taken on the responsibility of personally working for change.

The destruction of the Civil War could have led to a true Reconstruction of American society, but citizens and lawmakers North and South failed to make it work. Civil rights for blacks had been derailed. But in two generations, the movement would once again be on track.

IMPEACHED

"Is the respondent, Andrew Johnson, President of
the United States, guilty or not guilty of a high
misdemeanor as charged?"
SUPREME COURT CHIEF JUSTICE SALMON P. CHASE,
COMMENTING JOHNSON'S IMPEACHMENT TRIAL

n 1867, the hope of Reconstruction was still alive for the
Radical Republicans of Congress. They had gained control
of the Southern states. Only one thing stood in their way:
Andrew Johnson.

Now the Radicals decided it was time to do something that had
never been tried before in the American government. They decided
to *impeach* the President—or formally charge him with crimes that
could remove him from office. Some Congressmen tried to prove
that Johnson had plotted with John Wilkes Booth to assassinate
Lincoln. Their "proof," however, was discredited.

On March 2, 1867, over Johnson's veto, Congress passed the
Tenure of Office act. The act prohibited the president from getting
rid of any cabinet member or other officeholder without the
senate's consent. Johnson believed the act was unconstitutional.
And he desperately wanted to get rid of secretary of war Edwin
Stanton, who constantly supported the Radicals against the president. So, in August, Johnson challenged the law. "It is impossible
to get along with such a man in such a position," he said, "and I can
stand it no longer."

Johnson fired Stanton and replaced him with the popular General Ulysses S. Grant. But Grant did not serve for long. He was afraid that, under the Tenure of Office Act, he might be fined $10,000 or put in jail for five years. The Radicals suggested that they could be helpful to him in 1868, when Grant hoped to run for the presidency. So Grant resigned and passed the key back to Stanton, who locked himself in his office and refused to leave. Still Johnson would not back down. He ordered Stanton dismissed again and appointed General Lorenzo Thomas to the position.

The Radical Republicans had exactly what they needed. On February 24, 1868, members of the House of Representatives met to discuss impeachment. Johnson was called the "great criminal of our age and country." He was called "an ungrateful, despicable, besotted, traitorous man." At five o'clock the legislators voted. The vote was 126 to 47—to impeach President Johnson. Impeachment means officially accusing a president of crimes. It was the first time in American history that a president had been impeached "for high crimes and misdemeanors." When Johnson learned that he was being impeached for violating the Constitution, he exclaimed, "Damn them! Haven't I been struggling ever since I have been in this chair to uphold the Constitution they trample under foot?"

On March 13, 1868, the impeachment trial of Andrew Johnson began. Johnson's name was called, but he did not appear. Though the trial ran for weeks, Johnson never once set foot on the floor of the House to hear the charges or to speak on his own behalf. And his lawyers advised him to give no interviews to the press. Johnson was often frustrated when he felt his lawyers did not answer a question as well as he would have himself, and he often threatened to go in and speak for himself. But in the end he heeded his lawyers' advice. While the trial dragged on, he continued to tend to his presidential duties calmly and with dignity.

The vote was at last scheduled for May 12. One of the senators was sick, however, and so the vote was delayed until Saturday, May 16. The people of Washington could think of nothing else. Would the president of the United States be convicted of crimes? Or would

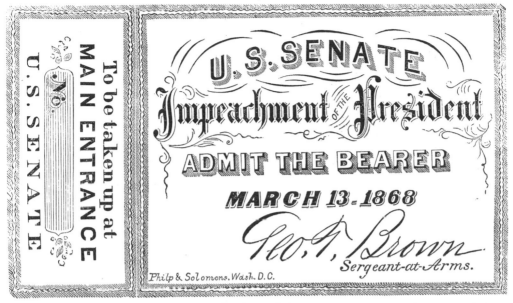

The trial to impeach President Andrew Johnson was as much a spectator event as a political one.

Johnson be acquitted? How would this senator or that senator vote? No one knew for sure what the outcome would be.

Finally the day of the vote arrived. It was a beautiful, sunny spring day. People poured into the streets and gathered on the steps of the Capitol building. The Senate galleries were overflowing with excited spectators.

At last voting began. The clerk called the roll. "Mr. Senator, how say you? Is the respondent, Andrew Johnson, President of the United States, guilty or not guilty of a high misdemeanor, as charged in this article?"

"Guilty."

One by one, in alphabetical order, the names were called and the votes cast. A two-thirds majority—36 votes—was needed to convict the president of the charges.

The final vote was 35 votes to convict, 19 votes to acquit. Johnson was acquitted—cleared of the charges—by a single vote, cast by Senator Edmund G. Ross of Kansas. The Radical Republicans had failed.

Colonel William Crook, the president's bodyguard, ran from the Capitol all the way down Pennsylvania Avenue to the White House. He rushed breathless into the library, where Johnson sat with friends. Johnson took the good news calmly as his friends gathered round to shake his hand. But tears streamed down his face.

Then Crook ran upstairs to Eliza Johnson's room, where she sat in her rocking chair, quietly sewing. "He's acquitted!" Crook cried. "The President is acquitted!"

"Crook," she said, rising to grasp his hand, "I knew he would be acquitted; I knew it."

A single vote spared Johnson from conviction at the impeachment proceedings held by these congressmen.

LAST DAYS IN THE WHITE HOUSE

"It is a victory not for myself but for the
Constitution and the country."
ANDREW JOHNSON, FOLLOWING HIS ACQUITTAL
AT HIS IMPEACHMENT TRIAL

outherners celebrated Johnson's acquittal with fireworks
and gunfire. Southern Unionists feared for their lives, and
some even left the country. Thaddeus Stevens declared, "I
see little hope for the Republic." Others in the Senate, however,
believed the vote safeguarded the presidency. The strength and
stability of United States democracy came from a sharing of power
among the presidency, the Congress, and the judicial branch of the
government. What would happen to this balance of power if
Congress could easily remove from office a president it disagreed
with?

Johnson was pleased with the outcome. Deeply ambitious, as
always, he began to believe that he might be able to win re-election
in the fall of 1868.

In June, he vetoed a bill that would readmit a "reconstructed"
Arkansas to the Union. Of course, it had been one of Johnson's
goals to readmit the Southern states. But he still objected to the
Reconstruction Acts and Congress's terms for readmission. On the
same grounds, he also vetoed a similar bill to readmit North
Carolina, South Carolina, Louisiana, Georgia, Alabama, and
Florida.

But these states, with new constitutions in place, were now in the hands of Republicans. Congress was eager to have their votes in the fall election. And so Congress overturned both Johnson's vetoes, and the states were readmitted to the Union.

In May, the Republicans had nominated General Ulysses S. Grant for president and Schuyler Colfax for vice-president. The convention also passed a Republican platform that called for black suffrage in the South but not in the North. And it declared that it fully approved of the impeachment of President Andrew Johnson.

Johnson was still hoping to win the nomination for re-election. He had been acquitted at his humiliating impeachment trial—but only by one vote. He could not forget those 35 votes that had called him guilty. He believed that winning the party's nomination—and re-election by the people—would completely vindicate him once and for all.

Johnson chose the Fourth of July to grant full pardon to all former Confederates except those leaders, such as Jefferson Davis, who were under indictment for treason. He also sent supporters to boost his candidacy at the Democratic convention, which opened in New York on July 7. Johnson was delighted by the convention's platform, which he felt supported his Reconstruction policies. It began by declaring that "the President of the United States, in exercising the powers of his high office and resisting the aggressions of Congress upon the Constitutional rights of the States and the people, is entitled to the gratitude of the whole American people" and thanked him for "his patriotic efforts in that regard."

But Johnson had alienated too many people in the Democratic party. After several votes, the party chose Horatio Seymour, wartime governor of New York, to run for president, and General F. P. Blair as its vice-presidential candidate.

Meanwhile, Thaddeus Stevens was continuing to dog the president. Stevens was 76 years old. Thin, pale, and weak, the senator continued to attend each meeting of Congress, even though he had to be carried up the long steps of the Capitol building to his seat. And he remained Johnson's enemy till the end. On July 7, he had introduced three additional articles of impeachment against Johnson. "The block must be brought out and the axe sharpened; the only other recourse from intolerable tyranny is Brutus' dagger." It was his last challenge to the president; Steven's died on August 11. Congress never took action on any other articles of impeachment, but the threat would always hang over Johnson's head.

The Republican convention and Stevens's final charges left Johnson bitter as he faced the last months of his presidential term. As the fall presidential election drew near, violence broke out across the South. Black and white Republican leaders were threatened. Political meetings were disrupted by violence. And the Ku Klux Klan used violence and murder to try to end Republican influence. Arkansas congressman James M. Hinds was assassinated. Three members of the Southern Carolina legislature were killed. Hundreds of blacks were murdered.

The Klan was effective in terrifying voters and keeping many from the polls on election day. But in November, Grant still won the election. It had been only four years since the election of Lincoln and Johnson. And yet Grant faced a nation perhaps more divided than ever before.

On Christmas Day, 1868, Andrew Johnson issued the last proclamation of his presidency—and succeeded in infuriating the Senate once again. This time he granted a full pardon—without restriction—to all Confederates, including President Jefferson Davis.

A few days later, Johnson celebrated his 60th birthday at a party for his grandchildren—and nearly 300 of their friends. Even Eliza, unwell as she was, came down from her rooms to watch. Flowers filled the rooms and the Marine band played, as the children of both Democrats and Republicans made the White House their playground. Johnson was probably not surprised, however, that General Grant did not allow his children to attend.

During the last months of his term, Johnson had continued to fight Congress over the policies of Reconstruction. Once he said in exasperation to Crook, "Everybody misunderstands me. I am not trying to introduce anything new. I am only trying to carry out the measures toward the South that Mr. Lincoln would have done had he lived."

The following March, on the day of Grant's inauguration, Johnson's staff seemed eager to leave for the ceremony. The president was at his desk. "I think," he said quietly, "we will finish our work here without going to the Capitol." That afternoon Johnson quietly left the White House. He and his family were going home to Greeneville.

17

WELCOME HOME, ANDY

"My few remaining years shall be devoted to the
wealth and prosperity of my country..."

ANDREW JOHNSON

Thousands of people lined the railroad tracks as Johnson's train crossed the Tennessee border. Eight years earlier, Johnson had fled Greeneville as a huge "Andrew Johnson, Traitor" banner stretched across Main Street. Today 15,000 friends and neighbors cheered his return beneath a banner that read "Welcome Home, Andrew Johnson, Patriot." He ended his speech that day with words of England's Cardinal Wolsey—a man who had lived through that country's civil war two centuries before:

An old man broken with the storms of state
Is come to lay his weary bones among ye,
Give him a little earth for charity.

But the former president was not content simply to rest his "weary bones" and enjoy a quiet life in Greeneville. He immediately went to work repairing the family home, which had been taken over and used as a barracks and a hospital during the war. Before long he turned again to politics. In 1869, he ran for Congress, hoping for a vote of confidence from the people of his

113

state. He was defeated. He ran again in 1872 and lost once more. Meanwhile, he watched Grant's administration fill Washington with scandal and corruption. Grant's cabinet was "a sort of lottery," he said, "those getting the best places that paid the most... from $65,000.00 down to a box of segars."

In 1873, an outbreak of Asiatic cholera in Tennessee sent many wealthy people fleeing. Johnson and his family chose to stay and help nurse the sick of Greeneville, where nearly 100 people died. Johnson himself became seriously ill with the disease. He recovered, but would never totally regain his health.

In 1875, Johnson won enough support to do something no other ex-president had ever done: He was elected to the U.S. Senate. A crowd rushed to the Tennessee capitol to hear his farewell speech. "I will go to the Senate," he said, "with no personal hostility toward any one.... My few remaining years shall be devoted to the weal and prosperity of my country which I love more than my own life."

On March 5, Andrew Johnson quietly entered the Senate chamber where only seven years earlier his name had been dragged through an impeachment trial. Many of those who had voted to impeach him were dead or had been defeated for re-election. After he took the oath of office, the chamber suddenly rang with cheers and applause. A bit embarrassed, he went to his desk and found it covered with camellias. A page offered him another bouquet and brought a blush to his usually impassive face. As friends gathered round to shake his hand, tears glistened in his dark eyes. Not long after his return, the *New York Nation* said of Johnson, "His personal integrity is beyond question and his respect for the laws and the Constitution made his administration a remarkable contrast to that which succeeded it."

Johnson made only one speech, on March 22—a three-hour attack on President Grant's administration. Two days later, the session adjourned and Johnson went home to Tennessee.

On July 27, Johnson went to spend a day with his daughter Mary Stover at her farm. Eliza was already there, and the family enjoyed a happy, leisurely meal together. That afternoon, he went upstairs to the guest room to take a nap. His little granddaughter Lillie followed him. After an affectionate little chat, Lillie turned to go. Something crashed to the floor. She turned to see her grandfather lying helpless on the carpet. Johnson had suffered a stroke.

The family helped him to bed, but Johnson refused to allow them to call a doctor. He lay in bed and talked quietly about his childhood in Raleigh, his life in the tailor shop, his political career. The next day he suffered a second stroke, which left him unconscious. On July 31, 1875, Andy Johnson died.

Johnson's family carried his body back to Greeneville to be buried. He had once said in a speech, "When I die I desire no better winding sheet than the Stars and Stripes, and no softer pillow than the Constitution of my country." And so he was buried on a gentle hill overlooking Greeneville, wrapped in the flag of the Union, a copy of the Constitution beneath his head.

This drawing accompanied newspaper accounts of the last hours before Andrew Johnson's death.

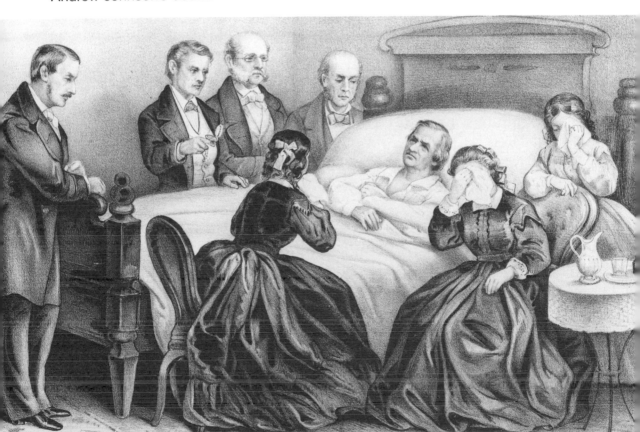

Epilogue

harles Dickens, the great English novelist, once visited the White House and later described Andrew Johnson, 17th president of the United States, as "a man with a remarkable face, indomitable courage and watchfulness, and a certain strength of purpose. I would have picked him out anywhere as a character of mark."

Born into extreme poverty, Andy Johnson became an apprentice and excelled at a trade that would take him far beyond his humble beginnings. Introduced to reading, he struggled to read for himself the words of the world's greatest minds. He taught himself the useful art of speechmaking. And he dared to have ambition.

Johnson's life was filled with contradictions: He was a tailor who became a president. A working man who rubbed shoulders with the elite. A Southerner who stood by the Union. A Unionist who ruined his career by defending those who had rebelled.

Andrew Johnson was an honest man who found his religion not in the words of Scripture, but in the guarantees of the Constitution—the only president ever humiliated by an impeachment trial.

Andrew Johnson had begun his presidency with great optimism. He had hoped to lead the nation quickly through its time of healing. He never wavered in his belief in the Union, the Constitution...and the people.

Perhaps the greatest achievement of his career was his compassionate pardon of Confederates in that first hopeful summer following the Civil War. His greatest disappointment: his failure to carry out Lincoln's dreams for a speedy, peaceful Reconstruction of the nation—and his inability to win the most important "debate" of his career.

"I don't know anything more depressing," he once said, "than for a man to labor for the people and not be understood. It is enough to sour his soul."

ANDREW JOHNSON

December 29, 1808	Born in Raleigh, North Carolina
1827	Married to Eliza McCardle
1843	Elected to the U.S. Congress
1853	Elected governor of Tennessee; serves two terms
1857	Elected to the U.S. Senate
1860	Announces in the Senate that he will be loyal to Union in the event of civil war
1861	Confederates fire on Fort Sumter in South Carolina; the Civil War begins
1863	Battles of Lookout Mountain and Chattanooga force rebels out of Tennessee; Union government is restored in the state
1865	The Civil War ends
	Elected vice president of the United States
	Sworn in as President of the United States after Abraham Lincoln's assassination
1868	Impeachment proceedings begun against Johnson in the Senate; he is later acquitted of all charges
1874	Becomes first former president ever elected to the United States Senate
July 31, 1875	Dies near Carter Station, Tennessee

SUGGESTED READING

Goodman, Walter. *Black Bondage: The Life of Slaves in the South*. New York: Farrar, Straus & Giroux, 1969.

*Kent, Zachary. *Encyclopedia of Presidents: Andrew Johnson*. Chicago: Childrens Press, 1989.

Marsh, Carole. *Out of the Mouths of Slaves*. Bath, N.C.: Gallopade, 1989.

Paley, Alan L. *Andrew Johnson: The President Impeached*. Charlotteville, N.Y.: SamHar, 1972.

*Stevens, Rita. *Andrew Johnson, Seventeenth President of the United States*. Ada, Ok.: Garret Educational Corp., 1989.

*Readers of *Andrew Johnson: Rebuilding the Union* will find these books particularly readable.

SELECTED SOURCES

ANDREW JOHNSON

Bacon, G.W. *The Life and Speeches of Andrew Johnson*. London: Bacon and Co., 1865.

Dickinson, John N., ed. *Andrew Johnson, 1808–1875: Chronology, Documents, Bibliographical Aids*. Dobbs Ferry, N.Y.: Oceana Publications, 1970.

Stryker, Lloyd Paul. *Andrew Johnson: A Study in Courage*. New York: Macmillan, 1929.

Thomas, Lately. *The First President Johnson: The Three Lives of the Seventeenth President of the United States of America*. New York: Morrow, 1968.

Trefousse, Hans L. *Andrew Johnson, A Biography*. New York: Norton, 1989.

Winston, Robert W. *Andrew Johnson: Plebeian and Patriot*. New York: Holt, 1928.

THE CIVIL WAR

Catton, Bruce. *The American Heritage Picture History of the Civil War*. New York: American Heritage/Bonanza Books, 1960. (1982 edition.)

Catton, Bruce. *The Civil War*. New York: American Heritage Press, 1971.

Catton, Bruce. *Reflections on the Civil War*. New York: Berkley, 1982.

Davis, Burke. *The Civil War, Strange and Fascinating Facts*. New York: Fairfax, 1982.

Foner, Eric. *A Short History of Reconstruction, 1863–1877*. New York: Harper & Row, 1990.

McPherson, James M. *Battle Cry of Freedom*. New York: Ballantine, 1989.

Index

Cathy East Dubowski has written more than 25 books for children, including *Robert E. Lee and the Rise of the South* and *Clara Barton: Healing the Wounds*, also in this series, and the Random House "Step into Reading" books *Pretty Good Magic* and *Cave Boy*, which her husband Mark coauthored and illustrated. Born in Virginia, she grew up in small towns in Virginia and North Carolina, then earned a B.A. in journalism from the University of North Carolina at Chapel Hill. After living for two years in Richmond, the capital of the Confederacy, she moved to New York City, where she worked for eight years in book and magazine publishing. Now living once again below the Mason–Dixon line, she feels her heart will always be somewhat divided between North and South—a fact she hopes adds a certain balance to her writing about the Civil War. She currently works as a writer and editor in Chapel Hill, North Carolina, where she lives with her husband and five-year-old daughter, Lauren.